Scratch My Itch

Scratch My Itch

A Caregiver's Honest, Humorous, and Healing Stories about the Horrors of ALS

Cyndy Mamalian

RESOURCE *Publications* · Eugene, Oregon

SCRATCH MY ITCH
A Caregiver's Honest, Humorous, and Healing Stories about the Horrors of ALS

Copyright © 2024 Cyndy Mamalian. All rights reserved. Except for brief quotations in critical publications or reviews, no part of this book may be reproduced in any manner without prior written permission from the publisher. Write: Permissions, Wipf and Stock Publishers, 199 W. 8th Ave., Suite 3, Eugene, OR 97401.

Resource Publications
An Imprint of Wipf and Stock Publishers
199 W. 8th Ave., Suite 3
Eugene, OR 97401

www.wipfandstock.com

PAPERBACK ISBN: 979-8-3852-1091-6
HARDCOVER ISBN: 979-8-3852-1092-3
EBOOK ISBN: 979-8-3852-1093-0

VERSION NUMBER 06/19/24

CORNER OF THE SKY (from Pippin) Music and Lyrics by STEPHEN SCHWARTZ © 1972 (Renewed) Stephen Schwartz All Rights Administered by EMI BMPC CORP. (ASCAP) and JOBETE MUSIC CO., INC. All Rights for JOBETE MUSIC CO., INC. Controlled and Administered by EMI APRIL MUSIC INC. (ASCAP) Print Rights for EMI BMPC CORP. Controlled and Administered by ALFRED MUSIC All Rights Reserved Used by Permission of ALFRED MUSIC

WALKING HER HOME. Writer Credit: Mark Schultz © 2003 Crazy Romaine Music (Administered by Music Services) All Rights Reserved. ASCAP

To protect the privacy of certain individuals in this book, their names have been changed.

This book is lovingly dedicated
to my mother, Barbara.
May her name serve as an
everlasting blessing to watch
over everyone who knew and loved her.

"It is always hard to see the purpose in wilderness wanderings until after they are over."

—John Bunyan, *The Pilgrim's Progress*

Contents

Preface | ix
Acknowledgements | xi
Introduction | xiii

1. Barbara 101 | 1
2. Angels Among Us | 14
3. Anna | 18
4. The Trifecta | 20
5. The Hoyer Lift | 25
6. Is It Contagious? | 27
7. In the Trenches with Friends | 29
8. Can You Hear Me? | 33
9. Scratch My Itch | 36
10. Climbing Stairs | 39
11. The Caregiver's Prayer | 43
12. Wine and Jellybeans | 45
13. Grasping at Straws | 48
14. Namaste | 52
15. Feeding Tubes Are Gross | 54
16. The Lecture | 58
17. Possible Side Effects | 62
18. Pills and People Who Listen | 65

19	Walking Her Home: A Love Story	69
20	Unpacking	74
21	Eulogyland	80
22	Ode to the Commode	86
23	Mad Kitchen Skills, Persuasive Essays, and the Rock of Gibraltar	89
24	Shakespeare-Inspired Conundrum	96
25	One Nurse, Two Nurse, Three Nurse, Four	100
26	Pink, Berry, Plum Maybe, but Never Peach	106
27	Operation Comfort Food	108
28	Planting Trees	111
29	Searching for Heaven	116
30	Postscript: Stitch by Stitch	121

Appendix A: Caregiver Bill of Rights | 127
Appendix B: The Original Lecture | 129
Appendix C: Anticipated Funeral Action Items | 133
Appendix D: Eulogy | 135
Appendix E: Meditation | 142
Appendix F: One Year Later: My Wish List | 146
Bibliography | 151

Preface

THERE IS CLEARLY A right and wrong shade of lipstick for a person in a casket, the revolving door of home health aides is like a very bad version of the TV show *The Bachelor*, and an ALS diagnosis makes scratching an itch feel as frustrating and futile as putting in contact lenses while wearing mittens. These are just a few of the lessons I learned while caring for my mother during her battle with Amyotrophic Lateral Sclerosis (ALS), or Lou Gehrig's disease. There are books written by people with ALS about their personal experiences, textbooks that discuss the nuts and bolts of the disease, and books on the famous 2014 Ice Bucket Challenge campaign that raised $115 million dollars for ALS research. My story, *Scratch My Itch*, is different. This book of short essays is about what it was like to live with and care for my mother Barbara, who had ALS; her motivations as she did her best to manage the disease; our combined fears; and the resilience and humor I discovered during this experience. There are also essays about what happens when an illness ends and a person is left to clean up the mess, search for glimmers of hope, and rediscover reasons for loving life again.

Having lived through this disease experience, I have a unique perspective I hope will be helpful not only to other people whose lives have been upended by ALS but to any caregivers who are looking for good company while they care for another person. More than 65 million people, 29 percent of the US population, provide care for a chronically ill, disabled, or aged family member or friend during any given year. If you, the reader, are a caregiver of a person living through illness or any compromised condition, I know you don't have the time or patience for anything long or verbose, which is why the chapters in this book are brief on purpose. And I am brutally honest in my writing about my experiences and want you to feel empowered knowing you are not alone in what you may be thinking and feeling. You need to know others are celebrating the absurdity and laughing with you amidst the chaos and pain. Caregiver or not, this book is also a good read for anyone interested in another story of the human experience. May we all feel greater compassion for those who are ill, better understand and appreciate the challenges of caregiving, and celebrate the humor that is essential to surviving it all.

    Looking back, I am thankful I had the opportunity, with my father, to care for my mother, that I was by her side during the hardest time of her life, and she was by my side during the hardest time of my life. I have come to realize it was a gift we could be together in the way we were. But acknowledging the value of a particular gift does not minimize the toll it takes on your body and soul. And it does not mean you minimize the time it takes to heal. I have learned as a caregiver, extending yourself a little grace is critical, necessary, and appropriate. The world is not judging you, and you should not judge yourself. Being human is okay; it's all we can be.

Acknowledgements

I HAVE IMMENSE GRATITUDE for the many wonderful people in my corner who supported my need to write and encouraged me when I decided to tell my story. I am grateful to my husband Paul, and my children Alexandra, Matthew, and Juliette for being my greatest cheerleaders, tolerating my noisy typing, and for loving me as much as you do. I would not want to do life with anyone else. I am grateful to my father Charlie, for the exceptional love and care he provided my mother; for his setting such an incredible example for Paul, me, and our children; and for his giving his blessing in my sharing our personal story with the rest of the world. Heartfelt love and gratitude for my beloved sister Christina, with whom I have taken every step of this journey and who shares a level of understanding only sisters can share, and for my sister's husband Mark and my nephews Nicholas, Christopher, and Andrew for their abundant and enthusiastic love and support. Special thanks to my husband's brother Rafi, who is one of my favorite humans and loves and protects our family fiercely. Lee Kelley, I am so happy for the love, companionship, and adventures you and my dad have shared together and am so very grateful you found one another. To family and friends, far and wide, who over many years supported our family during my mother's illness, thank you for every ounce of love you shared with me and my parents.

Deep and heartfelt gratitude to the doctors, nurses, and aides who provided medical and personal care; Montgomery Hospice; the ALS Association; the George Washington University ALS

Acknowledgements

Clinic; and researchers who continue to search for a cure for ALS. And, to my friends Cheri Rogers, Yvette Rose, Stephanie Hampton, and Laura Stotz, I am sad we were in the trenches together, but grateful we were able to support one another in the way we did. I believe there are angels among us, and I am especially grateful for Angel Number Three, Anna Moretti. My pastors; fellow church ladies; Stephen Minister Louise; Faith, Hope, and Lunch group; and family of faith at Potomac Presbyterian Church, you are the greatest blessing, and I can't imagine life without the love and strength of my faith community.

I adore and love my local tribe of best girlfriends Marianne Beardall, Heather Davies, Caroline Lulli, Stacey Kane, Susan Pereles, Cheri Rogers, Rebecca Sawyer, Kelly Tyree, and Kristen Ward; living the day to day with you is a gift and I am so grateful you didn't tell me I was absolutely crazy when I said I wanted to write a book. Special thanks to Kate Epstein of epsteinwords for her incredible developmental edit, which helped me refine my story. Thank you also to the early readers of my manuscript: Nina Eldred, Anna Moretti, Bob Plumb, Louise Plumb, Sonia Russo, Rebecca Sawyer, and Kristen Ward. Your constructive and enthusiastic feedback was exactly what I needed to finish this book and get it print-ready. *Bethesda Magazine* and Bethesda Urban Partnership, many thanks for the essay award for my lipstick chapter, which encouraged me to keep writing. Wipf and Stock Publishers, thank you for the gift of publication; you made this girl's dream come true! And to coffee bean growers and wine makers around the world, thank you for the liquid sustenance I consumed over many years while writing.

Finally, thank you to my mother, for raising me with such love and devotion; for taking me to poetry classes when I was little and teaching me over my lifetime how exciting it is to write, edit, and tell a story; for trusting me and being my best friend; and for letting me know in her own divine way she has found her corner of the sky.

Introduction

AT THE END OF the summer, just days before America's holiday, when we take a break from our labors and celebrate a season of a successful harvest (we aren't really farmers), hearing three English letters "A–L–S" in sequence for the first time changed my family's life. It was my own personal JFK's assassination, Princess Diana's death, or 9/11 tragedy, when I was cemented in time and place, and made a forever memory. And may I add, hearing bad news while on a family vacation is inherently wrong. My family of five had just pulled into the driveway of the mint green beach house, and we were looking forward to a weekend in the hot sun and sand with best friends and cold beers, when I received my parents' telephone call. My father, sounding choked up, was calling to relay the consensus of the doctors that my mother had been diagnosed with ALS.

Crap! . . . Crap . . . Extra Crap.

Here's the honest and crazy thing though: I didn't even know what ALS was. The fact that all diseases are intrinsically bad fueled my elementary-level expletive reaction. I had only vaguely heard of this disease, and I certainly had no idea how bad this disease would be.

ALS, or Amyotrophic Lateral Sclerosis, is a group of rare neurological diseases that mainly involves the nerve cells responsible for controlling voluntary muscle movement in the human body. Now when I think about ALS and what this disease does to a person and a family, just uttering those three letters in sequence exhausts me. And the disease is maddening because no matter what you think you can do, you can do absolutely nothing except

Introduction

manage the progression and challenges of the disease at each of its stages. If you read the textbook on ALS, you learn there is no cure, that symptoms get worse over time, there are mobility challenges (loss thereof), speech impediments (oh hell, eventually you can't talk), and breathing issues (yeah, you can't breathe either), all while your brain is fully functioning. But the textbooks don't tell you about all the little stuff, which for the caregiver, when added together, can feel almost bigger than some of the big stuff.

So, I want to share stories with you about all the little stuff. In this book, there will be no medical references or directions on how to manage the disease. There won't be a roadmap for what you do first, second, and third after receiving a diagnosis. There will be irreverent humor, some bad language, strong emotions, and many authentic and uncomfortably honest stories. It's definitely a ride, so buckle up. And truth be told, ALS sucks, so my hope is to make you laugh a little amidst the realities of a very crappy disease.

Lou Gehrig

Amyotrophic Lateral Sclerosis (ALS) is often referred to as Lou Gehrig's disease, named after the famous American first basemen who played for the New York Yankees and who is still considered one of the greatest baseball players of all time. Elected to the Baseball Hall of Fame, Lou was a two-time most valuable player, a seven-time All Star, and a six-time World Series Champion. He sadly was also a victim of ALS, diagnosed at the young age of thirty-six. Upon his retirement from baseball, Lou received a standing ovation for two minutes following his famous speech at Yankee Stadium on July 4, 1939. "For the past two weeks you have been reading about a bad break [his ALS diagnosis]. Yet today, I consider myself the luckiest man on the face of the earth." Lou Gehrig expressed his love of baseball, his teammates, and his fans, and sadly passed away just two years later. For more information about Lou Gehrig, visit www.lougehrig.com.

1

Barbara 101

BARBARA WAS MY MOTHER, and this chapter is the very abbreviated story of her equally complicated and wonderful life prior to ALS. Knowing her history and especially understanding the love story between Barbara and her husband Charlie (my father) and appreciating the depth of their love and devotion to one another, and to my sister and me, is important, especially in the face of her devastating illness. Context is critical, and the context which is our family's history and relationships is what got us through the worst experience of our collective lives. It sounds cliché, but my mother was my best friend, and she was the coolest, sweetest, and bravest person I have ever known, and I am so excited for you to get to know her.

As a little girl, Barbara Sielinski had Shirley Temple curls and looked perfect in a Ukrainian dance costume. Barbara was raised by two loving working parents, who had fallen in love at a young age, courted long distance, and were married in the Ukrainian Orthodox Church. My mother's family was of strong Ukrainian stock, and life revolved around the church. My mom was the baby of the family, and my Uncle Peter was the big brother. My grandparents spent long days in Boston factories—my grandfather worked at a sheet metal company, and my grandmother, a box factory—and so my mother's grandparents who lived next door helped raise her. My mother grew up at 18 City Point Court, a classic South Boston row house which was raw immigrant territory and a predominantly Irish neighborhood at the time. While my mother and her family were far from Irish, both ethnicities were always happy to raise a glass, and my mother's household was no exception. Spanning two generations, her father and her grandfather were both addicted to alcohol, and it tainted much of my mother's childhood and young adulthood.

Her Ukrainian heritage was very much a part of her daily life. The family spoke fluent Ukrainian, everything they cooked and ate was Ukrainian, Ukrainian ceramics populated the kitchen cupboards, and every item in the house was embroidered in Ukrainian patterns—doilies, window treatments, sheets, pillowcases, tablecloths, and clothing. My mother created the most exquisite Ukrainian Easter eggs called *pysanky*, layers of finely drawn beeswax and vegetable dye, which are now cherished family heirlooms. Easter baskets filled with homemade *paska* (braided bread), kielbasa, horseradish, and beautifully decorated eggs were blessed by the priest every year. Church on Sundays was hours long, complete with incense, beautiful vestments, saints adorned with gold halos, and a beautiful choir.[1] She went to Ukrainian camps during the summer where she danced, or she stayed with her maternal grandparents in Rhode Island to spend time away from the city. It was the Rhode Island summers where my mother got her hands pecked when she collected eggs from chickens, slept on the front porch at night, caught her breath and breathed clean air, and escaped. She was a lover of nature and animals, the countryside, and anything creative.

My maternal great-grandmother "Busha," who immigrated from the Ukraine with a single steamer trunk, helped raise my mother. She always smelled like garlic and raw onions, as she ate one a day as one would eat an apple. We say she lived to be in her nineties because her blood was so clean! She was a firecracker, and

---

1. Church also included hard butterscotch candies my grandmother would feed me during the service when I would visit her as a child, mainly to keep me preoccupied so I would fidget less. I choked for the first time in my life on a butterscotch candy in church; it was that Sunday I learned what the word "choke" meant and that I did not like it.

at eighty years old, she was still climbing a ladder to the second floor of the rowhouse to clean out the gutters and fix broken windows. She cooked ham with cloves, which my mother tolerated (and I detested), and my mother loved sharing the story about how when I was an infant, Busha would hold me above her head and say in Ukrainian, as her gums absent any teeth glistened, that I would become the president of the United States, because what could be a more incredible opportunity in the world than that!

My grandmother Anna, who we affectionately called "Buni," my mother's mother, was an exceptional cook and despite working long daytime hours at the factory, cooked everything from scratch for the family as soon as she came home. She was famous for her homemade baked beans, horseradish, and Christmas fruit cake, which she began making each year right after Thanksgiving. I doubt my mother loved fruit cake much, since she never made it herself as an adult. Or maybe my mother doubted hers would ever measure up, so she decided not even to try. Or she knew it was my grandmother's specialty and with her it should so remain.

The City Point Court rowhouse in which my mother grew up was love in a depressed place. The banister to the second floor was smooth from years of wear but wide and dark and perfect. The kitchen was always warm, the product of food being cooked or the oven being turned on and dangerously left open to heat the house. Cream, red, and black plaid blankets covered the living room sofa to protect it from wear and tear, a classy upgrade from the plastic coverings of years prior. Every wall in the rowhouse had random cracks that seemed to meander, making fascinating patterns in the process.[2] My grandmother's black Asian-inspired jewelry box with the tiny dancer who twirled to music when the box was opened was haphazardly placed on her hope chest, which was usually covered with all sorts of clutter. There was not a lot of jewelry in it, but the box was shiny and beautiful nonetheless.

---

2. I remember sharing a twin bed with my sister when our family would stay overnight to visit. I also remember bullying my sister to sleep on the side of the bed that touched the wall because we were both terrified of the cracks!

Scratch My Itch

My strongest memory of my mother's childhood home was of the basement stairs, so steep, creaky, and unsafe to travel, and in the back corner of the basement, the only toilet in the rowhouse, the kind with the water box above and the chain pull to flush. My grandfather's pink plastic toilet paper holder with AM/FM radio pimped out the freaky basement toilet corner. Also in the terrifying basement were coffee cans filled with assorted treasures and money buried under floorboards in the basement, as banks were a foreign concept and not to be trusted. After my grandparents passed away and the rowhouse was sold, my mother and I wondered often about how much treasure was still buried in the basement and if anyone would ever find it.

The kitchen pantry was stuffed from floor to ceiling with food, most of it stale and stashed between mouse traps that were often full. There was an alley off the wallpapered kitchen at the back of the rowhouse, where clothes washed in the kitchen sink were hung to dry on the line. There was no bathtub or shower in the rowhouse, so my mother sponge bathed with water my grandmother heated on the stove and poured into a large steel round pail in the middle of the kitchen. With age and increased height, members of the family graduated to washing their hair in the kitchen sink. In the parlor, behind my grandfather's blanket covered recliner, lived his stacks of girly magazines, which he enjoyed in addition to his Ukrainian newspaper. When I first discovered the magazines as a child, my grandmother told me to leave them where I found them because they made my grandfather "happy." This was an immigrant South Boston rowhouse, teetering on the poverty line and filled with love.

When my mother was in high school and my Uncle Peter in college, my father, Charlie, entered the scene. My Uncle Peter and my dad were best friends and military Pershing Rifles Fraternity brothers, and it was not long before my mother and father began to date. Proms, military balls, and date nights. It is all documented in the most beautiful scrapbook my mother created during their early years together—menus from diners, tickets from drive-in movies, photographs, match books and plastic stirrers! My father was Armenian, the third of eight children, and was raised by his working-class parents who had immigrated to the United States as they escaped the Armenian genocide in 1915. My parents had a shared ethnic experience, which meant neither had to explain anything about their family to the other. All the expectations, customs, and eccentricities were naturally and innately understood.

Because of my mother's glamorous childhood, she made it her goal to get out. She was not born with a silver spoon in her mouth, but she knew what classy was and she wanted it. My grandfather told my mother she could attend college and study to become either a teacher or a nurse; she wanted to study art but quickly chose a degree in education since she fainted at the sight of blood. At Northeastern University in Boston, she was part of the Homecoming Court for two years, joined a sorority, and found close friendships with her new sisters, who remember her as being kind, quiet, and having an infectious smile with big dimples.

When my mother finished college, my father asked for her hand in marriage, but my father's service in Vietnam for one year delayed the wedding. Four years her elder, my father had already graduated college, completed his master's degree, boot camp, and signal officer training when he received his orders for his Vietnam tour. My mother desperately wanted to marry my father before he left for Vietnam, but my grandfather forbade his daughter to marry an officer who was on his way off to war for fear she would become a widow. My parents wrote to one another every day for the year they were apart, and sometimes more than once a day. They sent flirtatious cards to each other, my mother sent innocent sexy photos to my father, and my dad sent back photos of military life in Vietnam. Their airmail love affair was the stuff of movies, and they were counting the minutes until they would be together again. I will confess, I know this because when I was a teenager snooping around inside my mother's closet, I discovered their letters, which made a lasting impression on me about what true love and romance looks like. Thankfully, my father returned from war, just weeks before their scheduled nuptials.

Scratch My Itch

The wedding, in looking at photos, was picture perfect. Barbara was the beautiful, elegant bride, and Charlie was the handsome, dashing groom. The fact that their photos are circa 1960s and many in black and white makes them even more iconic. An Orthodox ceremony in the church was the highlight of the day, with hand-braided crowns of greenery, crowns of self-sacrifice, which is what is required of both parties in marriage. They shared the communion cup, from that moment on knowing they would share everything in life—joy *and* sorrow, bearing one another's burdens. An Orthodox tradition, they joyfully and reverently walked around the altar three times, like a dance, their first steps together as a married couple. The reception I remember, as if I were there. My grandfather told my mother, "It may be your wedding, but it's my party" and he meant it. There was live music with two bands, ethnic dancing—both Ukrainian and Armenian, a wine bottle on every table, and an open bar (which was not typical for an immigrant family back then!). In this order, my grandfather "Gigi" (1) enjoyed drinking; (2) really liked a party with drinking; (3) enjoyed being loud, a showman, and in charge of the conversation; (4) enjoyed being a clown (figuratively and literally; he was in the Mason's clown group and would visit children in the local hospitals and make balloon animals); and (5) he loved being a host. This was *his* night to shine!

My parents settled in New Jersey, which is where my father was stationed post-Vietnam and post-wedding as he completed his two-year active-duty obligation and then found his first civilian job, and my mother spent her adult life creating and keeping a home that was completely opposite to that in which she was raised. There were no mouse traps needed in her house! Neat and clean to a fault, she made sure there was never any dust to be found, food that was a day past its due date was sent to the trashcan, and home décor was for the first time influenced as much by art as it was by necessity. As newlyweds, they got a parakeet and then a purebred puppy, both a far cry from South Boston's pigeons and stray cats. My mother happily taught elementary school until she was pregnant and ready to give birth, at which point she put her teaching career aside to raise her family.

But teaching for my mother simply went from the classroom to her own children. She stayed home to raise us, and that time in our lives was idyllic but not lacking obstacles. I love the photo that shows me as a months-old infant who could not even hold up her own head with her neck, being fed formula with rice cereal, while my mother was smoking cigarettes and drinking a cocktail!

Overall, however, life *was* idyllic. My mom made my sister and me hot breakfasts of Farina cereal, oatmeal, pancakes, or French toast, or we enjoyed boring dry cereal with milk. Occasionally, we were allowed to pick out a box of sugared dry cereal at the grocery store, which we proceeded to eat in a single sitting because it was such a treat and we lacked any semblance of self-control. She packed our lunches, home was safe and fun, and there were freshly baked cookies when we got off the school bus at the end of the day. Sometimes in lieu of homemade cookies, I would raid my mother's hidden Oreos stashed in the back of the kitchen cabinet that I was not supposed to know about. I learned a valuable lesson the day I lied to my mother, claiming I had not eaten the Oreos when I had, failing to realize the chocolate in my teeth had given me away. My mother's lectures were like kryptonite, and the Oreo debacle taught me the misfortune in lying and that my mother was always one step ahead of me. We would talk about our day, celebrate accomplishments, hash out dramas and middle school tragedies ("the years of tears"), and were empowered to believe we could rule the world. We were the *Free to Be You and Me* generation where feminism was increasingly celebrated; I still remember my parents giving me a beach towel that had a graphic of a little girl wearing a baseball cap backwards with the words "Never underestimate the power of a woman." There were no tasks around our house young ladies could not do, including shoveling the driveway, mowing the lawn, taking out the trash, and working with tools. My parents were desperately trying to teach my sister and me that we could be anything we wanted to be and do anything we wanted to do. Simultaneously, however, were also the messages that one day we may want to get married and have children, and we might want to select a career that will accommodate that choice. And at the forefront of all the instructing was the advice that we would want to go as far as we could in school because education is *everything*. As an adult now, with children of my own, I respect my parents for what they taught us. They understood life then and wanted us to be as empowered and equipped as possible to be our best selves in the world into which we were born.

My mother's adult life was filled with many mundane experiences and some incredible opportunities, both of which made her truly happy—the mundane *and* the incredible. She was, without a doubt, the chief operating officer of our home, supporting my father in his telecommunications career and his many business ventures. In addition to laundry, cooking, and cleaning, she managed the kids and any animals we brought home that we insisted would make great pets; we lived in the country, so the list was long, including frogs, salamanders, turtles, kittens, rabbits, snakes, fireflies, and butterflies to name a few! She and my father loved home improvement projects and creating together—best friends tending to their fruit trees and garden, making jam or Armenian string cheese, and pickling vegetables. My mother was an active parent volunteer during my sister's and my school-aged years, including leadership positions within the PTA and keeping her finger on the pulse of every schoolteacher and academic activity. She baked cookies for the school faculty at Christmas, chaperoned field trips, and did Ukrainian Easter egg demonstrations for our classes. She was the parent who called the school when she learned one of the teachers was throwing chalk at students from across the room and igniting his cigarette lighter by our heads when we did not answer questions quickly enough. A teacher by profession, my mother felt that type of classroom management was less than copacetic!

When we attended the Armenian Apostolic Church during my formative years, she was always helping in the church kitchen, with the annual bazaar, and she chaired the cookbook committee, publishing a beloved book and making wonderful new girlfriends in the process. When we later attended the Presbyterian Church in our hometown, she loved nothing more than singing in the choir (I think she appreciated that the words they were singing were English and not Ukrainian *or* Armenian!), ringing bells, and volunteering regularly at the local soup kitchen. Her favorite anthem was Martin Shaw's "With a Voice of Singing," which is the most uplifting composition. She was the mother who attended every football game in support of her daughter who was marching on the field during the halftime show. She was also the mother who was driving her other daughter one hour each way into New York City every Saturday morning for cello performance classes at The Julliard School. She was the mom who always showed up.

Barbara played in the Mendham Recorder Consort and loved performing early music, teaching herself everything she needed to know to play multiple recorders (sopranino, soprano, alto, tenor, and bass) and perform with an ensemble. It is in the Ukrainian DNA, and also tradition, to embroider, and my mother passionately loved this art form. She spent hours making the most beautiful embroidery floss masterpieces, and her passion for needlepoint was infectious, as she eagerly taught her friends, and my sister and me, the best stitching techniques. And her childhood love of Ukrainian dancing was generalized to a variety of dancing styles she learned as an adult including Armenian, Greek, and ballroom dancing. My mother was creative, a self-starter, and she never hesitated to teach herself how to do something she did not yet know how to do. "Idle" was not in her vocabulary.

Barbara's adult life was also filled with challenges that made her less than happy. Whenever my father's career hit a speed bump and it changed the status quo that was my mother's happy life, she became, well, less happy. She had worked so hard to build a beautiful life that was so different from the one in which she was raised that any pause in my father's career was reason for full-on panic and desperation. Job changes were reasons for panic. Moving to a new place was reason for panic. She was my father's best cheerleader and had immeasurable confidence in him, but the desperation she felt when things went wonky was too much for her many times. And yet, she was a fighter, and so she would work to survive. After twenty-three years out of the professional work force, my mother went back to work as a teaching assistant to help support the family. This reentry was followed by the realization that she would like to work in a special education setting, which led her back to school, and she earned her special education teaching certificate. My mother's second teaching career lasted over twenty-five years before she retired in 2010, and she was awarded Teacher of the Year in 2005–2006. When she passed away, in expressing his condolences, the principal of her school shared with us that Barbara was "truly loved, totally respected, and a once in a lifetime master teacher who was extraordinarily talented, patient, and loving toward those who so needed to be loved." Those words meant the world to us, and we prayed she knew this is how people felt about who she was and the work she did.

My mother was a beautiful woman who emerged from a concrete, factory-infused jungle in South Boston. She was not an esteemed diplomat, affluent philanthropist, powerful world leader, or famous entertainer. Her face never graced the cover of *People* magazine, nor was she ever quoted in *The New York Times* or *The Wall Street Journal*. She was never the byline on the ever-popular evening news. She was just a regular person. A regular, amazing person. A survivor. An artist. An active volunteer. A loving, compassionate, gifted teacher who touched the lives of so many children who needed a friend and mentor. The most fun, loving, devoted, and supportive spouse and mother who took those roles as seriously as if she had been an esteemed diplomat, affluent philanthropist, powerful world leader, or famous entertainer. She was also sadly a woman who died at the age of sixty-nine, a victim of ALS, which seems unjust when she was doing so much good in the world. But as Archbishop Desmond Tutu reminds me, "Dear Child of God, I am sorry to say that suffering is not optional."[3]

---

3. Tutu, *God Has a Dream*, 71.

Barbara as a young girl with her dimples and Shirley Temple curls.

Barbara at Northeastern University in Boston, Massachusetts.

Barbara and Charlie taking their wedding vows and wearing crowns of self-sacrifice.

2

Angels Among Us

It's funny how God finds a way of letting us know we are not alone in our struggles and challenges. I have learned He sends angels. The country music band Alabama sings about these angels: "They come to you and me in our darkest hours, to show us how to live, to teach us how to give, to guide us with a light of love."[1] In my case, the angels I came to know were not the kind with feathery wings and halos, although given their immense generosity of spirit, I don't doubt they secretly had those. In my case, the angels were actual real-life humans whose lives had been touched by ALS and who were able to provide words of wisdom, show me emotions I would eventually experience, and demonstrate that life does goes on. I had only remotely ever heard of ALS, or Lou Gehrig's disease, prior to my mother's diagnosis. After her diagnosis, it was as if at every turn, the disease was in my face, mocking me for being so naïve and ignorant. And God placed in my way people from whom to learn, understand, and empathize. Serious worldly angels.

It was not long after my mother was diagnosed that her symptoms started to progress rapidly. In just a few months' time, she went from having a slight foot drop, to being in leg braces, to not being able to go up and down stairs, to not being able to stand for any period of time without falling, to slurred speech, to not

---

1. The song "Angels Among Us" was written by Don Goodman and Becky Hobbs, recorded by the band Alabama, and released in December 1993.

being able to use one of her arms/hands. And so, our family made the decision to move into a different home that in addition to our family of five, would accommodate my parents and be handicapped accessible. Really, what happened was my mother did not like any housing options we considered (e.g., single family home nearby, condo nearby, over sixty-five plus housing nearby) until my husband Paul said, "Well, maybe you should just move in with us." Bingo! My parents worked quickly to pack up and sell their house in New Jersey and move to Maryland. We worked efficiently to find a new home, list and sell our house, and move one town over to a bigger place with an in-law suite.

With listing a home and moving comes all sorts of headaches. You must "declutter" your house before showing it for sale, which when you have three children under the age of nine and two cats (one of whom is diabetic and pees around the house) is a logistical nightmare. You must pack up as much as you can on your own because God knows, moving companies are expensive. And you need to contract with a moving company to move all the big stuff and the boxes you have pre-packed, praying of course they don't break anything because, FYI, it's not insured if you pack it yourself.

God introduced me to Angel Number One.

I was sitting across the table from one of the moving companies I was interviewing (Side note: I had no idea I was going to have to interview moving companies, but I did. I had to get estimates from them, and in a thirty-minute meeting try to assess just how much they would care about my stuff [i.e., not break it all]). So here I was in an interview with the moving company we will call "Capitol." Making small talk after discussing how little furniture we had and how many boxes we had, the nice Capitol representative asks me why we are moving. I tell him my mom is sick and my parents are moving in with us.

Capitol Rep: Oh, sorry, what is she sick with?

Me: ALS, Lou Gehrig's disease.

The room was completely quiet. Like the cricket chirping kind of quiet. Finally, he says, "My mom died of ALS."

Scratch My Itch

And there you have it. My first interaction with a person whose life had also been touched by ALS. If I can describe the feeling, I imagine it's much like being the only red-headed person on the planet, and then you see, for the first time, another red-headed person. Or you are the only person in the world who has ever hiccupped, and then you see for the first time another person with the hiccups. Or you are an alien, and for the first time, you realize there are life forms on other planets. You get it. It is *that* kind of stop your heart from beating, choke on your saliva, not know what to say next kind of feeling. And I am pretty sure I just stared at this lovely Capitol representative for endless minutes, with nothing but a glazed over expression. And then we got talking. And I quickly saw a grown man transform from New York gruffness to gentle, vulnerable, and sad within minutes. And that was my first glimmer of what ALS does to a family member. It renders them helpless but compassionate. Even though he had already lost his mother, and my mother had just been diagnosed, we shared an unspoken bond. We hired this moving company because I knew we would be in good hands.

Not many weeks later, we were out to dinner with one of my husband's colleagues and his wife. It came up in conversation that we were planning to move, the reason being to accommodate my parents and my mother's new diagnosis.

Colleague: Really, oh, I am so sorry, what does your mother have?

Fair question. My response: ALS, Lou Gehrig's disease.

Quiet. Like the cricket chirping kind of quiet. My husband's colleague then shared that his father died of ALS. God placed in my way Angel Number Two. We talked about the disease, and I learned from Angel Number Two that the disease is so maddening the person with the disease will eventually want to commit suicide and may ask you to help in that process (holy shit, it gets that bad?!). From that dinner on, I kept waiting in fear for that moment when my mother would ask me to help end her life.

Finally, God sent Angel Number Three. Anna was introduced to me by a best friend, who when she learned of my mom's diagnosis said, "You need to talk with my friend Anna. Her mother died of ALS, and Anna now works for hospice." I had her email address in hand, but it was not until we were a year into my mother's illness when I finally reached out. And Anna was the most angelic of all the angels.

3
Anna

Doing her best flight attendant impersonation, my new friend Anna advised me a year into my mother's illness: "Put your oxygen mask on first, Cyndy." It was the mantra by which I forced myself to live during those remaining two years.

There are some very important events in our lives when we actually *forget* all the little details. I find it extremely frustrating that years later I cannot remember the exact words in a conversation, what I was wearing, and all the delicious particulars. I remember only the take home points and the big picture but not the nuances and specifics of an event. I don't remember much about my initial meeting and conversation with Anna. I remember being in a restaurant booth. I remember barely eating. I can't tell you what season it was or whether I was in Ugg boots or flip-flops. I don't remember whether I had showered even once that week, although if I were meeting someone outside the house, I pray I had. But what I do remember is being able to, for the first time since my mother had been diagnosed, talk about what was scaring me most and ask all the seemingly inappropriate questions I had about the disease but had not been able to ask anyone else. Anna answered each question honestly. She helped me understand the progression of the disease. She helped me understand what I would need to do to survive, even as my mother was barely surviving. She helped me plan for different levels of care, different challenges within the disease, and helped me understand the extent to which this disease was going to wreak havoc on my family. She was the only person I felt I could ask the "how will she eventually die?" question. And Anna told me exactly what would happen. She did not mince words, she did not sugarcoat anything but was honest and spoke with integrity and compassion—and ironically hope. This was the greatest gift anyone could have given me at that moment in time. That I remember.

In keeping with the "my memory sucks" theme, I can't tell you exactly how many times I reached out to Anna over the next two years looking for guidance and clarity in moments of desperation or pure panic. I know it was not less than a half dozen and not more than a dozen. But what I do remember is that she was there every time with her quiet confidence and deep compassion. And she was there at the end when I needed her support most of all.

> Hey Cyndy . . . off we go [on the 75-mile ALS Express Bike Ride]. Be assured I will carry Barbara's name with me and will be thinking of you. Anna
> —Email Anna sent me ten months after my mother passed away

4

The Trifecta

ALS, Lyme disease, and cancer. Oh hell, throw in a spiral fracture for fun! The well-known adage "when it rains, it pours" most certainly applies to my mother's situation. And really, it makes no sense. This was a woman who exercised regularly (she even kept an exercise journal), ate mostly healthy foods, and spent her adult life taking regular recipes and making them "light." And yet her body was beholden to multiple diseases. No sense. The lesson I take from this experience is we should all eat whatever the hell we want and not worry about being the healthiest versions of ourselves. Disease clearly does not discriminate.

Shortly after my mom was diagnosed with ALS and she moved into our new home, she fell. This happens with ALS patients. Their muscles can no longer support them as they walk, and they go down. And when they fall, they go down hard. When my mother fell in the bathroom, although clearly in immense pain and clothed in panic, she was desperate we not call the paramedics because that was admitting vulnerability and setting herself up for embarrassment as she was only partially dressed, was without makeup, and her hair was not done (when the strong handsome emergency personnel come to your house, you want to put on the dog, do you not?). She insisted, between crying and moaning, she would "be fine," the pain would "eventually go away," and she would be vertical in no time. It was a good thing we ignored her

The Trifecta

pleas, did not try moving her on our own, and called for help. It turns out my mother had a spiral fracture to her leg, which was thankfully operable. The salt in the proverbial wound, however, is that when you are an ALS patient, they skip operating because they know you eventually won't be able to walk. Swallow that pill. Given her progressing ALS, the doctors suggested it would be less invasive and less traumatic to cast her leg and let the bones heal on their own and we agreed. They ultimately sent my mother to a rehabilitation facility so she could begin the healing process and get used to her new, even greater compromised condition before coming home.

And all sorts of new activities grace your personal schedule when you are in rehabilitation and you can't walk. You use a breathing machine to keep your lungs expanding and contracting at optimal levels; you do exercises in bed to maintain range of motion for the limbs that are working; and you are taught self-care techniques, like how to use dry shampoo, since you can't be in a shower (and if we are being honest, the bedhead hairstyle looks good on no one except maybe model Cindy Crawford). And the clincher: you learn how to use a bedpan. Using a bedpan sounds like it should be a small feat since it's a bit like sitting on a mini-toilet, but in bed. For my mother, learning to use a bedpan was pretty much like climbing Mount Everest. And in fairness to my mom and all other bedpan users out there, I concede there is nothing fun or comfortable or private about bedpans. Everyone knows your most awful business, and in short, bedpans suck. *But*, when you are a person with ALS who eventually will not be able to walk, a bedpan is a critical piece of the daily maintenance puzzle, and you need to embrace the pink plastic mini-bowl because you need it. There is a bedpan learning curve for everyone—the person on the pan and the person who must deal with the gift the person on the pan has given you. We can all admit we glance to see what we have shit into the toilet, but we don't really enjoy looking at it. Seeing and managing someone else's adult-sized undiluted waste that is within arm and nose's reach is even less enjoyable. Wiping an adorable pint-sized baby's bottom is sweet grossness. Wiping the

Scratch My Itch

adult ass of a person, even a person you love, is amplified grossness. You understand, so let's move on. None of it is glamorous.

When a person gets the death sentence of ALS, they do pause often and wonder if their symptoms could possibly be explained by absolutely anything else, because most anything else offers a potential solution. This wondering, of course, is fueled by the fact that there is no single conclusive test to diagnose ALS. Doctors typically rule out everything else it could be, and when they have exhausted all the other possibilities, the ALS diagnosis is made. So, amid ALS, spiral fractures, and bedpans, my mother started doing research to see if there could be any other explanation, other than ALS, for the symptoms she was experiencing. She had done her research and learned that chronic Lyme disease can mimic symptoms of ALS, so she asked her doctors to run some additional blood work. She was hopeful what she had was Lyme disease and not ALS. You see the psychology here. And her instincts were correct; she did have Lyme disease! The doctors attacked the Lyme disease head-on with high doses of antibiotics, and my mother tried assorted home remedies, only to find mild improvement with some symptoms while the majority of her ALS symptoms continued to worsen. Extinguishing that small glimmer of hope for my mother was the start of an even deeper depression.

And as if my mom were not having enough fun already, she had to undergo a colonoscopy because we found blood in her stool (I hate this word, by the way: "stool" . . . no matter what word we use to describe what it is, it just sounds gross. Apologies to all reading.). We had discovered a large hemorrhoid (another ridiculous word!) when caring for her, but those are common; we threw a little Preparation H at it and waited for the medicinal magic to happen. Turns out it was not a hemorrhoid; it was a big fat ugly tumor. So, all you sports fans, if you are keeping score that is four for "shitty diagnoses" (ALS, Lyme disease, spiral fracture, anal/rectal cancer) and zero for "life is awesome"! I don't know about you, but that score makes me want to vomit, crawl under a rock, and never come out, which is exactly how my mom felt. But my mother, who had not completely lost her will to live and still had hope simmering somewhere in the deep recesses of her heart, had a chemo port put in, underwent eight weeks of daily chemo and radiation to shrink the tumor, and endured horrific radiation burns so the tumor could be safely removed. She did not want to die from cancer if her ALS could be cured.

But wait, there's more! If you order now, you can get an extra set of steak knives for free! My parents' life was starting to mimic a TV promotional advertisement. The high-pressure sales pitch for ALS and the deal sweetened with other diagnoses that just kept coming, one right after the other. My mother spent four days in the hospital for a sepsis infection. She then had to be admitted to the hospital for about five days over New Year's for a huge blood clot that extended three-quarters the length of her leg. The doctors had to put in a stint and my mother added blood thinners to her list of daily medications. We could not sing "Auld Lang Syne" quickly enough and bid farewell to the past year. But happy new year to us! During an annual physical and after some routine blood work, my father was diagnosed with multiple myeloma, which is a cancer within the bone marrow. I think at this point we were all thinking we were going to need that extra set of steak knives to put ourselves out of our collective misery. Long story short: my father started an experimental treatment through the National Institutes of Health, and we were suddenly balancing doctors' appointments, treatment protocols, medicinal regimens, side effects, and the personal care of two sick people in a very short period—and in small quarters. We were running on empty, fuses were short, and my parents and I were exhausted.

I cannot offer you some morsel of contentment and inspiration here. The diagnoses that were piling up were exhausting for both the people receiving them and the person caring for them. I found during this time of diagnostic turbulence, I turned to excessive amounts of dark chocolate and red wine—and a Bible verse in Rom 5: "Not only so, but we also rejoice in our sufferings, because we know that suffering produces perseverance; perseverance, character; and character, hope; and hope does not disappoint

Scratch My Itch

us . . ."[1] In all honesty friends, dark chocolate, red wine, and hope were *my* trifecta. Those three things did not disappoint.

> Dear God, thanks for all the interesting experiences today. Alex burned her leg on an exhaust pipe, Babi broke her leg, why do you let this stuff happen? Fix it. Amen.
> —My son Matthew's nighttime prayer, eight years old

---

1. Romans 5:3–5 (New International Version).

5

The Hoyer Lift

MY KIDS SAW THE new contraption in our arsenal of ALS equipment and their first response was "*cool!*". It is literally a device that makes you fly. Each kid took a turn in the sling, trying to show their grandmother what a fun and amazing new acquisition this was for our family. "You can fly, Babi!" And really, what is not cool about that?! Everything, when you are a sixty-nine-year-old woman with ALS.

A Hoyer Lift is a large metal contraption with a sling that helps you move a person from Point A to Point B, from the bed to the wheelchair, for example. People with ALS, despite weight loss, are heavy dead weight. So heavy. As the disease progresses, they cannot help you in any way as you move them since they cannot move their muscles. Eventually, they cannot even hold up their head. Which means, unless you are built like the Hulk and can scale tall buildings in a single bound like Superman, you need help to move your person from Point A to Point B. The technology is technically simple—just put the person in the sling and then crank the sling into the air so they can be flown to the next location, at which point you crank them down into their new real estate and remove the sling (really, it is a large metal base with wheels). I wish I had a photo of my mother in the Hoyer Lift so you could appreciate just how simplistic but terribly useful this apparatus was—but Hoyer Lift moments were not Kodak moments. I thought the Hoyer Lift transfer would be easy peasy lemon squeezy; it never was, technically or emotionally. We found it took two people to safely use the Hoyer Lift: one person to push the device from Point A to Point B, while a second person was managing my mother as she sailed through the air in the sling. We also discovered flying is only fun when you feel like you have some control and independence in the matter, which the person with ALS does not have. They cannot get themselves safely and comfortably into the sling; they cannot brace themselves as they move; they cannot move their arm or leg so it does not hit a wall or door frame; they cannot turn their head to anticipate the next turn or what is ahead. Essentially, the person with ALS is dependent on the pilot, and they are flying blind, which makes the Hoyer Lift terrifying and definitely not cool.

Looking back, one of the first pieces of equipment I wanted out of the house after my mother passed away was the Hoyer Lift. I detested it, in part, because it was very large and hospital-grade ugly and just took up too much space in an already crowded bedroom (did I mention it was just super ugly?). But I detested it mostly because, while it did help us with my mother's care, her visual and vocal expressions of fear, panic, and exasperation whenever we used it to move her always broke my heart. She could barely put words together, she was struggling to breathe when even slightly reclined, bed sores made the sling all the more uncomfortable, and she was flying through the air unable to control any part of her body or the experience. Vulnerability is raw, and ALS patients have no shortage of it. Apologies to my children, I know you thought the Hoyer Lift was the best thing ever, but cool does not trump love.

6

Is It Contagious?

Living with someone who has a terminal illness for which there is little known opens up a big old can of "Crap! Is it contagious?!" and you are left wondering if you will get it too. While ALS is not contagious in the conventional sense—there is no "ALS germ" that travels through the body—it may be genetic. Researchers know very little about ALS and its causes, but current research suggests that in 5 to 10 percent of cases, ALS *is* genetic. And that possibility is petrifying. Of course, with those odds, I could also get hit by a bus tomorrow. But when a loved one is faced with a horrific terminal illness, we all become part of the "Me Generation" and pray we are not a part of that 5 to 10 percent.

When my mother visited the ALS Clinic at The George Washington University, she participated in several studies that helped the clinicians in their study of the disease. Not clinical studies, where they were testing the success of one treatment or intervention over another, but rather, studies where they were gathering biological, historical, and environmental data that would help them better understand the etiology of the disease. And this included genetic testing. Seemed simple and truly benign at the time. It was just a blood test. But then I remember the doctor asking me, "Would you like to know if the ALS your mother has is genetic?" Is it genetic? Genetic?! That is a *big* fucking question, and it was asked so nonchalantly! Do I want to know if I will suffer like she is suffering?

Scratch My Itch

Do I want to know if I will die like she is dying? Short answer? Hell *no*! In the flight or fight scenario, I was pushing past doors, jumping over furniture, leaping tall buildings in a single bound to get away! I was the ostrich burying her head in the sand in hopes of never having this conversation ever again. And then my rational side took over, and the internal conversation between my rational and irrational went something like this:

> Rational Me: The doctor asks a reasonable question.
>
> *Irrational Me:* The hell she does!
>
> Rational Me: Wouldn't you like to know the science behind the disease? Whether you are genetically predisposed to have this disease?
>
> *Irrational Me:* Hell no! Wait, why would I want to know?
>
> Rational Me: Knowing in advance whether you are genetically predisposed will help you ... will help you ... oh shit, yeah, it won't help you ...

Here is the thing. I declined to know whether the ALS my mother had was genetic because really, what was the benefit in knowing? Based on current science, there is no cure. Based on current science, there is no cost-effective/time-effective method of slowing the disease. Knowing I was predisposed for genetic ALS would simply be a dark cloud I would wake up under every day, wondering if today I would feel the first tremble in my hand or misstep and fall off balance for the first time. Whether today, when I looked at my children, I would worry they too would suffer and eventually die from ALS. *No thank you.* I decided I would rather risk getting hit by the bus. The Route T2 bus goes through our town every day.

7

In the Trenches with Friends

I AM GOING TO go out on a limb, and assume we are all familiar with the famous sentiment "misery loves company," written by seventeenth-century English naturalist and botanist John Ray. Incidentally, Ray is also credited with the phrase "blood is thicker than water," which my parents threw around often during our formative years as they taught my sister and me the value of family allegiance. Who knew a seventeenth-century botanist would be such a quotable guy? But I digress. The point is, I am not quite sure I ever gave considerable thought to what the phrase "misery loves company" means. Was Ray suggesting that people who are miserable get some consolation or solace in knowing other people are miserable too?

I can't say that while suffering through anything in my life, I have ever felt better knowing someone else is simultaneously suffering. I can acknowledge however, there is value in the *support* you find through others who are suffering while you too are suffering or through others who are caretaking while you are simultaneously caretaking. Sharing war stories, resources, and lessons learned while in the trenches with friends does offer some consolation and strengthens friendships. As Archbishop Desmond Tutu observes, "We don't really get close to others if our relationship is made up of unending hunky-dory-ness. It is the hard times, the painful times, the sadness, and the grief, that knit us more closely together."[1]

During my mother's illness, two dear girlfriends were also supporting their parents who had neurologically based terminal illnesses[2] and were struggling with the challenges of caregiving. We shared contractor phone numbers so modifications could be made to our homes like ramps, shower platforms, grab bars, and special new door hinges that make the door open wide enough to accommodate a wheelchair. We shared bits of knowledge we gleaned from our individual interactions with disease-specific associations, doctors, and other professionals who were supporting our parents through their illnesses. One of these girlfriends, while caring for her own mother, set up a dinner delivery schedule for our family for the three weeks my mother was in the hospital and rehab when she broke her leg. Knowing I would barely be home during that time to cook for my children, she could appreciate what would be most helpful to me because she was living the dream at the same time. Most importantly, we gave each other the opportunity to bitch, moan, cry, and laugh, a special sorority of women who were in the trenches of hopeless caregiving together.

After my mother passed away, two more friends' lives were steamrolled by ALS. One girlfriend was suddenly caring for her father, and another girlfriend was in shock caring for her thirty-six-year-old boyfriend. And then in getting to know a new friend, I learned she had just lost her older sister to ALS. It seemed the disease with three letters was again mocking me at every turn. This time, I put on my battle armor, and found consolation in knowing I could be the one to share what I had learned during my mother's illness and prepare my friends for all that was ahead as they navigated the disease and their eventual recovery as caregiver. I felt sad they were going to become sisters in our special sorority without

---

1. Dalai Lama, et al., *Book of Joy*, 111.
2. One parent had ALS like my mother, and one parent had multiple system atrophy (MSA), which is a rare, degenerative neurological disorder affecting your body's involuntary (autonomic) functions, including blood pressure, breathing, bladder function, and motor control.

In the Trenches with Friends

Greek letters but welcomed them with open arms and certainly no hazing. With all the humility I could muster, I hoped this time around, *I* could be the angel.

When I consider Ray's "misery loves company" sentiment, I have to believe he was not implying people, when miserable, love the company of other people who are miserable because they find some bizarre joy in the suffering of others. Instead, I am inspired by and drawn to the Dalai Lama's perspective: "We realize that not only do we suffer, but so do many of our human brothers and sisters. So, when we look at the same event from a wider perspective, we will reduce the worrying and our own suffering."[3] Douglas Abrams, who interviewed the Dalai Lama, writes, "I was struck by the simplicity and profundity of what the Dalai Lama was saying. This was far from 'don't worry, be happy,' as the popular Bobby McFerrin song says. This was not a denial of pain and suffering, but a shift in perspective—from oneself and toward others, from anguish to compassion—seeing that others are suffering as well. The remarkable thing about what the Dalai Lama was describing is that as we recognize others' suffering and realize that we are not alone, our pain is lessened."[4]

It was a beautiful spring afternoon at a local park in May 2015, and students ages kindergarten through eighth grade from our small private Episcopal school had just finished a fun-filled and athletically challenging field day. Each student was decked out in red and white shirts, shorts, face paint, ribbons, hats, and tutus—school pride and sportsmanship at its finest! And the day concluded with a wedding. My friend and her thirty-six-year-old boyfriend who had rapidly progressing ALS, both teachers, had decided to get married. And given their penchant for the non-traditional, they decided field day was the perfect opportunity to do so. Our little school community came together to make this moment as tender and special as possible for them. As the bride walked down the hill to meet her groom, she wore a black sundress with white daisies; muck boots; and a white lace, tulle, and floral

---

3. Dalai Lama, et al., *Book of Joy*, 37.
4. Dalai Lama, et al., *Book of Joy*, 37.

fascinator on her head. Students who flanked both sides of the grass-strewn aisle handed her flowers one at a time, creating the perfect bridal bouquet bloom by bloom. Parents and students together hummed Wagner's "Bridal Chorus," the simplicity of which rivaled the music of the finest church pipe organ. The bride and groom shared quiet vows that had even deeper meaning given the challenges ahead. "I will fall down with you. I will stand up with you. I will grow with you." It was honestly a tie as to whether there were more celebratory child-blown bubbles in the air or tears falling from every pair of eyes that watched. It was a moment that allowed every person there to express joy for the moment it was and compassion for the couple who was preparing to face their worst nightmare together.

Like Douglas Abrams, I too was struck by the Dalai Lama's words. In feeling compassion for others who suffer, we feel less pain. We become less focused on our own misfortune, and instead focus on supporting others who are struggling. I think this is what happens when you are in the trenches with your friends, haphazardly thrown into the places and situations where we are doing difficult work at the same time. We extend compassion to one another, and in so doing, our own pain is lessened. That sounds like the work of angels to me.

8

Can You Hear Me?

HUMANS ARE FUNNY. I sometimes believe when we don't fully understand a situation, we fill in the blanks; we make assumptions at warp speed to make the situation we don't fully understand make more sense and ideally more comfortable *for us*. Every day, I saw these "fill in the blank" moments in how people spoke to my mother upon seeing her in a wheelchair, noting her limited mobility, and hearing her delayed speech. The fill in the blank assumption for people was this: if her body is delayed, her mind must be delayed as well. But this is a faulty assumption of ALS patients whose bodies deteriorate but whose minds stay sharp as a tack. Our experience, however, was that 80 percent of the time, people would crouch down, and speak slowly and more loudly to my mother as if she could not hear well or understand what was being said. Speaking in slow simple sentences...

> Barbara, . . . can . . . you . . . hear . . . me? . . . How . . . are . . . you . . . today?

I understand this phenomenon. It's the same thing that happens when someone whispers to me and my natural inclination is to whisper back. My mother would speak in delayed, difficult to understand words, and people would speak back the same way. This dialogue format was so frustrating and exhausting for my mother who was embarrassed people could not understand her.

She just did not have the strength to project her voice, and people could not understand her. And people mimicked the tenor of her voice. No one was ill-intentioned in talking to my mother in this manner. It is just how humans fill in the blanks.

Despite everyone's good intentions, however, I would watch my mother wind up, and then the fumes would start steaming from her ears as if in a Wile E. Coyote and Road Runner cartoon, until I could find a polite way to let the person know that her hearing and mind were fully intact, and they could speak normally. The million-dollar question, however, is how does one politely message that? I tried a few different strategies. My favorite strategy was interrupting the slow talker and immediately talking to my mother at a very rapid pace and more quickly than one would normally talk. It would sound a little like when you listen to a podcast at 1.2 or 1.5 speed. "Excuse me for interrupting, Patty. Hey Mom, you remember that time last spring when we went downtown and saw the art exhibit at the Smithsonian? Doesn't Patty's scarf remind you of that very large painting we saw? Same colors, same patterns! Really, so pretty, Miss Patty!" And my mother would nod her head the best she could and say "yes" as quickly as she could. We were leading by example. I spoke fast, and my mother not only tracked my fast talking but understood it and responded quickly. Our vaudeville act was usually enough to make the person doing the slow talking question the assumption they made and adjust. It was a rather magical strategy if I do say so myself.

Sometimes when my fast-talking message did not resonate and effect change, I would move on to strategy number two and would politely say, "Oh, you are so sweet. You can talk normally to my mom. She understands everything just fine. Her speech is just a little delayed." But oh, how I hated doing this, because it usually made the slow talking person feel bad. It did however, most often mean they did not make that faulty assumption again and would talk to my mother more normally the next time. Short-term loss, long-term gain?

My third and final strategy was to surreptitiously educate. I would somehow weave into the conversation a challenge my mom had recently experienced but then end on a hopeful note. "Unfortunately, mom has been having some new challenges with her left fingers and not being able to use the remote anymore. But this has not slowed her thinking down—still smarter than all of us put together! That is what makes this disease so difficult." Following my sleight of hand, more often than not, the person with whom we were talking was able to discern how slow talking and dumbing down the conversation was not necessary when talking with my mother.

In hindsight, while my speed talking strategy was absolutely more fun and I got quite good at it, this final strategy was probably the more compassionate and valuable approach because education is critical. Education ensures people are less naïve about this disease and more equipped to advocate for ALS victims. Education helps us ask important research questions so we better understand the etiology of the disease and can hopefully discover a cure. And most importantly, greater education means we have fewer blanks to fill in on our own and fewer Wile E. Coyote and Road Runner moments in life. This feels like an ideal goal, doesn't it?

9

Scratch My Itch

LET'S PLAY A QUICK game I often play, sometimes during the day, but most often when I am lying in bed at night. Pause, for just a minute, and think on the number of times today you rubbed the back of your neck and shoulders in hopes of getting that little bit of tension out, readjusted your stretched-out bra strap that slid part way off your shoulder, touched your ear lobe to feel your earring and make sure the back was still securely in place, or stroked the one day's growth of facial hair that predictably sprouted. Now think about the number of times in the past hour you rubbed your eyes, moved that stray piece of hair off your face, or wiped your nose. Finally, think on the number of times in just the past minute you readjusted your bottom in your chair or bed, touched your lips with your fingers, or scratched an itch. I constantly think about and appreciate the freedom of these types of small movements. I also have spent countless nights lying in my bed thinking about the twenty-five or more adjustments I make just to be comfortable enough, so I am able to embrace that deep slumber. And then I pause, and I apologize to my mother.

It is human nature to adjust our bodies in response to the multitude of annoying stimuli that are bugging us—the stray piece of hair, the itch, the dripping nose, the wrinkled piece of clothing that is just wrinkled enough in a single spot to bother the top layer of our skin and set our nerves ablaze. And we adjust. It is part of human mechanics. But a person with ALS can't adjust. They can feel the sensation, they are fully aware of the annoying or uncomfortable stimuli, but they can't move and adjust. And the challenge in navigating this part of human mechanics is compounded by the fact that the ALS patient loses their ability to articulate well and/or speak. If you add on top of that the fact that, for the majority of caregivers we were hosting in our home, English was not their first language, it makes it all the more complicated to communicate the myriad of adjustments the ALS patient wants made. You can begin to appreciate how scratching an itch becomes an even larger ball of yarn to untangle.

So, it became everybody's job—mine, my father's, my husband's, my children's, the caregivers'—to help navigate and manage this part of my mother's human mechanics. It was labor intensive. It was exhausting and frustrating. It was maddening. It was also guilt-inducing, because it was truly depressing to think about how miserable this part of my mother's reality was. I should have felt and shown nothing but compassion, and yet, I got impatient having to adjust her constantly. Real, honest to goodness "I am going to rot in hell" guilt.

One night, my father was out of town on business, and we had a new home health aide who had never met my mother in to help us. This aide could not understand a single word my mother uttered. Not a single word. I was up for most of the night taking care of my mother as the new aide helplessly watched. After that long night, and in my infinite wisdom, I devised a series of charts we attached to my mother's lap table, hoping she could point to directions as needed when people did not understand her. Directions, for example, that included itch on nose; pull butt toward dresser; pull butt toward closet; wipe nose, dripping; pull blanket up; pull blanket off; smooth sheets; pull hair off face; push shoulder toward closet; push shoulder toward dresser; raise feet; lower feet; raise head; lower head; move right hand onto leg and spread fingers; adjust top; pull sleeves down; align sleeve with shoulder and pull from underarm. You get the idea. Sadly, my mother poo-poo'd the charts, and they were only marginally helpful.

Scratch My Itch

As we play the game and think about how many movements we make consciously and unconsciously to adjust our bodies and respond to unpleasant stimuli, we are left with one very big question: How could a person not go absolutely crazy experiencing all of these sensations, wanting to make all of these adjustments to their body, struggling to communicate those needs and wants, and not be able to do so? It's a great question for which I don't have an answer. I do believe it is maddening for the ALS patient who is trapped in their body. And for the person whose job it is to make these adjustments 24/7 for the person for whom they are caring? Trying to anticipate the need, making the adjustment, and then learning it didn't really solve the problem, and needing to redo it repeatedly? Or chasing the itch that started at the base of the neck, but now is behind the ear, then on the eyebrow, and has at last settled in the corner of the eye? Being the body-adjuster-itch-chaser is a full-time job, and it too is maddening in its own sort of way. So really, compassion for both sides, each pulling on the rope in a metaphorical tug-of-war game.

To all those persons struggling with ALS or any other disease that limits your physicality, my heart breaks with you as you manage the challenges associated with your physical inability to adjust to all things that are bothersome. That reality is simply maddening and unfair. And to all you caregivers out there, I see your "rub toes" and "adjust pillow" and raise you one "pull disposable underwear from between butt crack" and "move legs from straight to frog leg position." Let's try to at least smile at the absolutely necessary and simultaneously insane adjustments together!

10
Climbing Stairs

STAIRS ARE A FASCINATING thing. Humans, in their infinite wisdom, decided living on the land, our feet directly on God's good soil, was not sufficient, and with increasing human density, we started playing with the concept of vertical real estate. But with no wings, we needed a way to ascend to a higher level, and so the original architects of our time developed a concept we call stairs (technically, the ladder came first, but I digress). As Webster explains, "a series of steps or flights of steps for passing from one level to another."[1] But humans are never satisfied, and we are also often lazy, so we invented stairs that move *for* us, saving us the effort of climbing! In 1892, the first escalator was introduced as a novelty ride at Coney Island, and then everyone realized its generalized potential! And in 1923, C. C. Crispen, a Pennsylvania entrepreneur and self-taught engineer, took the escalator to a higher level, in my humble opinion, and invented the precursor to the modern stairlift for a friend of his who was immobilized due to polio and was having trouble getting between the two floors of his home. A magical seat, if you will, that could take you up and down the stairs! Necessity is the mother of invention, is it not?

In 2015, our family became the proud owners of the Acorn 80 curved stairlift, "a solution that will make life easier for you"! It had

---

1. "Stair."

a built-in start and stop facility, a smooth and comfortable ride every time, a rechargeable battery pack, a safety belt (please tell me you too can hear the jingle in your head: "buckle up for safety, buckle up"), and folding storage capabilities, even on a curved staircase. Really, the list of accolades for this device goes on, and all for the bargain price of $9,000 and change. You can close your mouth. I know you are in awe of this incredible piece of technology and wish you had one too.

We were all pretty stoked about getting this stairlift installed in our new home for many reasons, and these are not in any particular order: (A) Technology is cool, and this contraption was amazing! It glided gracefully along its curved track, from the basement floor to the first floor. Hats off to the Coney Island escalator guy, but this was like having our own amusement park ride *in our house*, (B) It was considerably cheaper than gutting the front hall closet and installing an elevator, (C) My kids *loved* it. They could not wait to have their friends over to show off the cool moving seat that was now in their home (see A, and remember humans can be lazy), and (D) It helped us get my mother from the basement to the first floor of our house which was liberating for her and for us on so many levels.

Similar to the Hoyer Lift, my kids were first in line to try out the chair that moved up and down the stairs like the Haunted House ride in Disney World (but with no haunting). "Babi, this is *awesome*! You will love it!" In addition to riding the chair themselves, their dolls and stuffed animals took turns, they used it to send snacks between floors, and they had races to see who would get down the stairs more quickly—the person in the stairlift or the ball that was rolled down the stairs. My husband even used the chair to transport heavier items like a case of wine! You can begin to appreciate the value and potential this magical chair had!

My mom, however, did not love it quite as much. What they don't share with you in the stairlift promotional materials or the infomercials is *how* the really calm, composed, lovely person on the stairlift gets *into* the chair that moves and how they get *out*. Transfer at the bottom of the stairs was not a big deal. We were on solid ground, and we could transfer her from her powerchair to the stairlift chair and back pretty gracefully. At the top of the stairs, however . . . well that is an entirely different story. We had about three feet of space to fit her powerchair, and the transfer from stairlift chair to powerchair (and vice versa) was happening at the top of a set of very steep stairs. We had minimal room to maneuver, and it was precarious for all involved every time. Remember also, the ALS patient can't help at all in the transfer. Just solid dead weight. I am embarrassed to report the number of times my mom was almost tipped off the chair headfirst down the stairs. In hindsight, that might have been faster and easier.

And as if being buckled up in a seat that is traveling up and down the stairs is not humbling enough, we realized buckling my mother up at the waist was only partially holding her body in the chair. Since she could not control her upper body, she could and would . . . flop . . . forward or sideways—left *or* right! Obviously, traveling up or down the stairs in the magical chair flopped over, forward or to the left or right is neither comfortable nor safe. Our primitive solution was to strap her in all the more! We got one of my dad's leather braided belts and wrapped it around my mother's upper body, across her chest, and belted her to the chair back. We took "humbling" to the next level as my mother traveled the stairs buckled *and* belted.

This transfer happened at least once a day, sometimes more, depending on the day's activities. It was liberating for my mother and my father to be able to escape their basement living quarters, see more natural light, be a part of the hustle and bustle that comes with three young children, sit at the larger kitchen table, and be amongst the family. And while the transfer experience brought with it nail-biting terror at the top of the stairs, it was exponentially easier for me to manage my three children from the main floor than from the basement. I appreciated being able to spend time with my mom and dad while still being a present mother of three.

After my mother passed away, we did have the ever-helpful Acorn Company remove the stairlift from our basement stairs. It was a bittersweet moment. I think we all appreciated having a wider staircase again to climb in the traditional way, and while the stairlift was super cool and helpful, it was not terribly attractive, so like the Hoyer Lift, it was nice to get the ugly out of the house. But removing the stairlift was also another reminder my mother was no longer with us, which made it difficult to say goodbye to the magic chair. It had really been a ride to freedom for my mom.

But rest assured, the stairlift will be back. What we learned is that the stairlift was custom-built for our specific curved staircase, so it can't be used easily in any other house. It now lives in our basement storage closet, and one day, when my husband and I are older, when our knees have gone bad and the thought of climbing sixteen stairs is more than either of us can fathom (or we just want the fun amusement ride back in our house), I will call up the ever-helpful Acorn Company and have them put it back. The magical chair was and will always be a keeper!

11

The Caregiver's Prayer

ABOUT HALFWAY THROUGH MY mother's illness, I attended the funeral service of a friend's mother. During the service, the chaplain prayed this beautiful prayer:

> This is another day, O Lord.
> I know not what it will bring forth, but make me ready, Lord, for whatever it may be.
> If I am to stand up, help me to stand bravely.
> If I am to sit still, help me to sit quietly.
> If I am to lie low, help me to do it patiently.
> And if I am to do nothing, let me do it gallantly.
> Make these words more than words and give me the Spirit of Jesus.
> Amen.[1]

This was one of those deeply spiritual moments when I felt as if the prayer was being prayed for me, or more specifically, for my mom. It was clearly the prayer of a person with ALS. As the body continues to deteriorate, the person goes from being able to stand, to being able only to sit, eventually being able only to lie down, and then to doing nothing except think. And doing nothing when you can think fully requires a truckload of prayer if one is to do it at all, never mind gallantly. So, coming back from the service, and feeling so incredibly moved, I emailed my parents the prayer.

1. Episcopal Church, *Book of Common Prayer*, 461.

Scratch My Itch

I was expecting this prayer to move mountains, change lives, heal deeply. My father, God bless him, emails me back with his addition to the prayer, which would technically come before the amen:

> And if I should say nothing to keep the peace and to minimize confusion, give me the understanding and patience to do so.

And all God's caregivers said, "Amen."

12

Wine and Jellybeans

WHEN I WAS GROWING up, I thought jellybeans were the happiest pieces of candy on planet Earth. They were little, chewy, colorful, and sweet, and they came in my Easter basket every year. Over my lifetime, I have curated favorite jellybean colors, which coincide with favorite flavors. And as a child, I also knew my *parents'* favorite jellybean colors and flavors. My father loved red cherry-flavored jellybeans, and my mother loved black jellybeans, which was terribly convenient since black jellybeans were (1) ugly and (2) a gross licorice flavor. My mom just loved them.

And jellybeans, like many things, can go from good to bad quickly, under the veil of ALS. There was a time toward the end of my mother's illness when before bed all she wanted was exactly eight jellybeans (four white coconut and four black licorice) *and* white wine.

The wine I understood. My mother came from a long line of alcoholics, including her father and her grandfather. When her grandfather was inebriated, he leaned more toward evil than good. When my mother was a little girl, her grandfather took her to the beach in South Boston, and in his inebriated state, he kept pushing my mother's head under the ocean water, holding her down, and she almost drowned. In her lifetime, my mother never again put her face in the water when swimming in the pool or ocean. She would not go back to that moment.

Scratch My Itch

But alcoholism runs in families and ours was no exception. My mother, knowing full well the evils associated with this disease, also drank excessively: first socially, and then to help numb daily stresses, disappointments, and unresolved sadness and pain. White wine was her go-to. When she was healthy, she would often start drinking while she was cooking dinner and continue until she was asleep. Hers was the fully functioning, excelling at great things variety of alcoholism. My mother had to detox for the first time in her life when, because of ALS, she fell and broke her leg and was in the hospital and the rehabilitation facility. They don't do happy hour there! While hospitalized, I knew my mother was struggling with missing alcohol when she began requesting milkshakes from Cheeburger Cheeburger, the hamburger and French fry restaurant across the street. In those first few days, she drank piña colada, Irish cream, and amaretto-flavored milkshakes, desperately hoping the shake would magically transform to the real deal. So, given that history, it was no surprise that at the lowest moment of her life, when she could barely move, talk, or breathe, she wanted wine before bed. Self-medication is a real thing.

Looking back, I now understand a little more about why four white and four black jellybeans were so important. My mother was advocating and fighting for control. When she could control little else in her world, her body, or her schedule, it was her way of spitting in the face of death, being able to chew something, anything, even if it took her ten minutes per jellybean. (You do the math. There were eight jellybeans and don't forget, sips of wine in between. It made for a damn long night.) And I was not always nice. I was bitter, tired, and angry she was being so selfish, and we were starting with eight jellybeans at 11:00 at night. Who gave a fuck about jellybeans?! My mother did, and now I understand why. Jellybeans were life.

> The jellybeans and wine were replaced with ice chips tonight. The demands are simple but painful so late at night. I imagine some day long in the future, we will laugh about jellybeans and wine, but right now, I secretly

Wine and Jellybeans

wish I could get her that glass of wine and feed her those jellybeans one at a time.
—Email I sent to a friend.

Please thank Alexandra for the tour of the photo album and Juliette for picking out the three best Jelly Bellies for me.
—Email from a friend after attending my mother's wake. We had bowls of jellybeans around the room with only her favorite flavors.

13

Grasping at Straws

How is it exactly in our day in age of living, when men and women travel to the Moon and beyond, when we are fully accustomed to the miracle that is the Internet, and when scientists have cloned a sheep, we have yet to know *anything* about what causes ALS or how we might cure it? When someone gives you a diagnosis with no options at all for a cure, just a simple "sorry, there is *nothing* we can do, but please check in with us every three months so we can monitor your journey to dying," it can make a person a little cranky, a lot depressed, and absolutely fucking frustrated. But it also makes that person first curious about and then determined to find a cure *on his or her own*. And so, the search begins for the ALS patient. "Surely there is a something I can do," they think. The human survival instinct kicks in big time.

My mother researched and/or tried all sorts of home remedies: hydrogen peroxide cocktails, hyperbaric oxygen therapy, expensive water purifiers that produce alkaline drinking water, rife machines that claim to cure diseases through vibration, and supplements from "pretend doctors" who claimed they could magically cure her. In addition, she added certain foods to her diet, removed other foods from her diet, prayed, stopped praying, and started praying again. And every time the ALS patient tries something new and it does not work, it is the equivalent of driving a car into a brick wall and climbing out of the wrecked vehicle. And after a few days of recovery, they convince themselves to get back into the driver's seat and do it all again. Because that is the human's want and need to survive.

What was so confusing and fascinating to me is my mother was clearly wearing an ALS cloak of many colors. One patch of the quilted coat represented the days she would tell me she was miserable beyond measure but grateful for the care she was receiving, another patch for the times she told me it would be easier for everyone if I just killed her, and another patch for the times she said she would like to take her own life. Yet next to these patches were the patches for the days she took supplements hoping to extend her life, another patch representing the number of websites she had searched in hopes of finding an obscure cure, and finally a patch for the many attempts she made to cure her disease given the lack of any scientifically proven medical options. I tried to be as understanding and patient as I possibly could with the myriad of hypotheses and off-the-grid cure regimens, but the degree to which these potential cures complicated an already hectic and exhausting care schedule made my impatience rear its ugly head more than once. The potential cure that bugged me the most was the hydrogen peroxide cocktail.

This was an H_2O_2 concoction my mother was supposed to drink on an empty stomach ("I must wait three hours after taking it to eat"), which just raised so many concerns for me. One, drinking hydrogen peroxide. Two, drinking hydrogen peroxide. And three, drinking hydrogen peroxide. For starters, the hydrogen peroxide bottle says "*Warning*: For external use only" followed by "If swallowed, get medical help or contact a Poison Control Center right away." Red flag? Anyone? In addition to my concerns about my mother ingesting hydrogen peroxide, I also had concerns about how we were fitting this "must be taken on an empty stomach" cocktail into the already compressed schedule of caregiving, providing nourishment through her feeding tube, taking supplements from the whack job pretend doctors, ingesting prescriptions from an actual medically licensed doctor, and wine and jellybeans. I asked my mother a couple weeks into the hydrogen peroxide cocktail schedule if she felt there had been any improvement. She was proud to report the sores in her mouth had gone away. Really?! Isn't that why some toothpaste and mouthwash products boast the benefits of hydrogen peroxide in their formulas? The hydrogen peroxide bottle says "swish around your mouth for one minute and then *spit out*" for a reason!

At times like this, when the regimen of home remedies is making you question every facet of illness and life, it takes a best friend to ask the honest question, "Cyndy, are you trying to poison your mother?" It was the question that needed asking, just so I could laugh at the absurdity because I would never poison my mother, and yet, ALS makes the absurdity feel rational and real. No, I was not trying to poison my mother. For starters, this was her idea alone, and we were just the hired help. But as my mother struggled to reconcile her condition with the lack of an available cure, I don't doubt she had done the math: it will either help me or kill me. Given the hell in which she was living, I believe she honestly felt she would be happy with either outcome.

A family member once noted how frightening it must have been for my mother to be faced with so much that was beyond her control. It was *horrifically* frightening for her, and whenever I tried to walk a mile in my mother's shoes to see what it felt like (the irony of course being she couldn't walk anymore), I too felt panicked, sweaty, and nauseous. Her depression over having ALS was so severe she did often talk about suicide, and much of this depression was of course linked to fear. She had read the ALS manual and knew what was ahead. And hydrogen peroxide cocktails aside, I never believed my mother would follow through with killing herself, nor could she without someone else's help because of how far her disease had already progressed. It was usually a statement made to remind us of just how horribly she felt and how scared she was. With the help of a psychiatrist, we finally convinced my mother to take a prescription antidepressant and a sleeping pill, both of which helped a little. But the magic medication does not take away the thing that is causing the pain, so it just meant she was a little *less* depressed and could get a *little* more sleep. The same relative who noted how frightening this all must have been for my mother also commented, "I often ask myself if I could handle the unknown with the dignity and feisty spirit your mom possesses." It was undoubtedly my mother's feisty side that fueled the hydrogen peroxide movement within the house for so long. But as my mother's ALS continued to progress and she saw no improvement with the daily H_2O_2 cocktail (and she hadn't died from taking it), she eventually stopped asking for it. And in a different way, that was frightening too.

14

Namaste

I DESPISE EXERCISE, ROUTINELY quip, "I only run if I am being chased," and while I feel good *after* exercising, it's the process I detest. I would rather be reading magazines, tending my garden, folding laundry, or cleaning toilets. And frankly, when one person is busy caring for another, self-care gets relegated to the bottom of the to-do list. I just did not have the energy—physical or emotional—to stuff myself into a pair of stretchy tight black leggings, a sports bra, and put on my running sneakers. Yet halfway through my mother's three-year battle with ALS, I decided to embrace exercise.

I spent minimal time contemplating what type of exercise I might do. Really, it all just sounded abhorrent to me. But, in reading *People* magazine regularly in the grocery checkout line, I learned *all* the stars are doing yoga, and if famous people are doing yoga and look good, and I want to look good, then I must do yoga; it is a simple "If A, then B" equation. So, while caring for my mother, I searched out the local yoga studio.

And yoga *was* good! It helped me breathe and feel empowered, and I was given permission to escape and hum. I owned a super cool Mediterranean blue yoga mat and an equally beautiful, embroidered yoga mat travel cover. I strengthened my body and mind in a publicly acceptable way, I felt strong, and then my mother died. I realized at that moment that no form of exercise, art, music, anything really, could replace my loss or make me feel

Namaste

strong. Emptiness was just emptiness, and nothing could fill it. And I found I could not reach for my yoga mat in the pretty travel cover with the same affection. Yoga is now on the backburner because I am not sure I ever genuinely loved it, and it was something I started during the worst time of my life. Psychology 101: Negative Association. But exercise is *not* bad, and I was determined to try again.

After my mother passed away, I humbled myself at a Zumba class. It's funny—in my mind I am still a sixteen-year-old girl with her 1980s high school dance club. Imagine the movie *Flashdance*, permed hair, leotards, leg warmers, barely developed bodies; we were so cool. And yet, in the wall-to-wall mirrors, I did not see cool. I was not moving quickly enough, and the parts of me that *were* moving weren't supposed to be moving. My dancing was awkward compared to the sexy instructor's merengue, salsa, and samba, and while the professionals did not break a sweat, I left every class looking as if I had just stepped out of the shower. Zumba ultimately hurt my knees, so my quest for tolerable exercise continued. I discovered the YMCA's heated indoor pool, and let me assure you, swimming at the YMCA was a *great* confidence booster! I conveniently swam during senior water aerobics, and at forty-five years old, I looked damn good compared to the eighty-year-old ladies splashing in the water!

My tasting menu exercise experience is not unique, and I have yet to find my favorite form of exercise. But I did learn the importance of caring for oneself when caring for another person. I had forgotten somewhere along the way that I was allowed, entitled actually, to care for myself at the same time I was caring for someone else. Despite the guilt I felt for taking personal time to exercise, it did not make me a bad person for doing so. And while it takes significant effort, and I personally despise it, exercise *is* good. As Elle Woods says in the movie *Legally Blonde*, "Exercise gives you endorphins. Endorphins make you happy."[1] Happy helps you survive.

---

1. *Legally Blonde*, DVD.

15
Feeding Tubes Are Gross

I CHOSE A CAREER in criminal justice for many reasons. For starters, beginning at a young age, my favorite literary genre was mystery. As a child, I loved the *Encyclopedia Brown* mysteries series, and I would read a *Nancy Drew* novel in a day, never putting it down. As an adult, I have always loved Patricia Cornwell or Carl Hiaasen novels which simultaneously entertain and challenge my intellectual sleuthing. In my teen and young adult years, I would most often pause my television channel surfing on shows like *Murder She Wrote*, *Matlock*, *Cagney and Lacey*, and *Law and Order*; I loved any story—the more sophisticated and complicated the better—where I needed to analyze data and evidence, and solve the whodunit. In college, my favorite class was Psychology and the Criminal Justice System, and I loved volunteering at the local domestic violence shelter and interning at the juvenile court. After college, while working at a residential treatment center for children and youth with mental disorders, I realized the clients who interested me most were the ones who were ultimately going to end up in the criminal justice system. Everything led me toward criminal justice, and *nothing* in my interests led me toward a career in medicine. Like my mother, I tend to grow weary and almost faint at the sight of blood and am squeamish beyond measure with most body-related issues and injuries. I selected social science for a reason.

Feeding Tubes Are Gross

And yet life loves to challenge us with experiences out of our comfort zone, which is why when my mother elected to get a feeding tube, I almost crawled under the covers of my bed, never to emerge again. Don't get me wrong, I emphatically agreed with her decision to *get* a feeding tube *and* encouraged it. As the ALS disease progresses, patients begin to struggle with swallowing, which directly affects their ability to eat and drink. And yet, we all know we need food or some form of sustenance to live and survive. Enter the revolutionary medical device called the feeding tube. She needed the feeding tube to continue living; however, it was not clear *I* was going to continue living after I saw it and whether I could maintain it.

A quick surgical procedure—the doctors attach a rubber tube that goes through your abdomen wall and directly into your stomach so you can pour nutrients into your body via the feeding tube, completely bypassing your mouth and esophagus. See? Revolutionary! You leave the hospital with a rubber tube about six to eight inches long sticking out of your stomach. Unfortunately, with any medical procedure there is always risk of something not working, which is exactly what happened in my mother's case. A few days after her procedure, when she went back to the surgeon to have the tacks removed (the tacks were what was holding her stomach together and the feeding tube in place . . . think really strong stitches), the doctor realized the balloon that keeps the feeding tube inflated had deflated. It was a defective balloon! So, my mother went back into surgery so they could put in a new balloon. *Long* story short, and one Kind Bar later,[1] my mother was sent home with a new feeding tube and my father, sister, and I were

---

1. A little unpaid product endorsement: during my mother's surgical procedure, my sister and I walked to the Whole Foods market next door to the hospital to grab some lunch. The market had a little display set up, and they were handing out samples of a new snack bar they were selling called a Kind Bar. I am a picky eater and generally don't just pop new foods into my mouth without careful inspection, but on this day, the stress of surgery had clearly melted my inhibitions, and I never considered *not* popping that medley of nuts, seeds, and fruit into my mouth. And I am so glad I did! It was heavenly! It was just one of those silly moments I will remember forever: the day I tried a Kind Bar and loved it! I still eat one every day.

Scratch My Itch

handed extensive instructions outlining what was required of us to feed my mother.

My criminal justice training did not help me at all in the feeding tube department. I can fully intellectualize and appreciate how feeding tubes are essential for prolonging the life of the ALS patient for whom swallowing food has become challenging, if not impossible. And I am grateful my mother had a feeding tube because it gave us many more months with her toward the end of her illness. But feeding tubes are, for lack of a better word, gross. Really and truly gross! We were required to clean the skin around the feeding tube so it would not get infected. We had to flush the feeding tube with water so it would not get clogged or backed up. We had to pour assorted concoctions through a funnel into the tube, which went directly into my mother's stomach, which did provide her the essential nutrients she needed to survive. But we also had to pray we were not pouring the liquid in too quickly because if it went in too quickly, my mother would feel sick and have terrible acid reflux and would want to vomit and/or the tube would back up and we would be cleaning up spilled liquid off my mother's stomach. Can you sense my queasiness? I am physically sinking slowly down in my chair, my fingers barely reaching the keyboard, as I type and describe this experience for you. It's a tube that projects out of your belly and goes directly into your stomach! When we were not using the feeding tube, we had to tape it to her body, rather than risk it being pulled out! Let me tell you what that did to my psyche every time I had to dress and move my mother. I was a hot mess.

In addition to the physical care and maintenance of the feeling tube, my mother's medication, supplement, and now feeding tube schedule was so complicated and ridiculous I had to write it out so we, or anyone else who was assisting with her care, could follow it, since it was becoming increasingly difficult for her to give directions and for anyone to understand what she was saying. I printed out a detailed daily schedule, with assigned times for absolutely everything, put it in a swanky three-ring binder and gave it to my parents for their review (because approval and buy-in are critical!). It was Draft Number One. Knowing my mother was a perfectionist, I knew it would never be final until about Draft Number Ten, and by then, she might even be dead. I did feel like I should get some credit for respectfully including in the schedule a time slot for wine and jellybeans, the time of the evening that was going to be the end of me. I know you are thinking a can of Ensure through the feeding tube pairs beautifully with a glass of wine! The joke, of course, is I also scheduled the day ending with lights out at 9:00 pm, which I knew would never, ever, ever, ever happen, ever (isn't that a Taylor Swift song?!).

What did I learn from this feeding tube experience? Not to state the obvious, but I learned feeding tubes are gross. More importantly, I learned I can do hard things. I also learned I still do *not* have a penchant for medicine. God bless the surgeons, doctors, nurses, and researchers who continue to push the medicinal envelope and discover treatments, procedures, and devices that improve quality of life and extend the lives of those we love. We need these smart and inventive people! I am so grateful for my mother's feeding tube and the extra time it gave us with her. Moving forward though, I am going to stick with Nancy Drew; she's the furthest thing from gross.

> The purist in me has grown weary. Tonight, I had to open a wine bottle with a corkscrew instead of a screw cap, and I was annoyed. That can't be good.
> —Email I sent to a friend the night I had to feed my mother through her feeding tube for the first time.

16

The Lecture

While managing my mother's multiple inflictions, we were also helping my father manage his disease called multiple myeloma, which is a cancer of the bone marrow. We thank Agent Orange for this gift. Just another part of the fancy swag bag Army personnel were sent home with after their service in Vietnam. And part of my father's experimental treatment included a prescription of steroids. I don't remember why the doctor believed steroids should be a pawn in my dad's disease treatment game but they were. What I quickly learned, however, is steroids really mess with a person and make them Captain Crunch crazy. You understand. You start your day with a smile, but then you are so jacked up on sugar, you are living on magical Crunch Island off the coast of Ohio and in the sea of milk, with talking trees, crazy creatures, a mountain of Captain Crunch cereal, and the roof of your mouth is ripped to shreds. Steroids are that kind of crazy. Research suggests that people who use steroids report more anger than nonusers, as well as more fights, verbal aggression, and violence toward their significant others.[1] Those researchers are correct.

    Steroids had a way of changing my incredibly loving, patient, funny, gentle, sweet father into someone we did not recognize. One night in particular, the steroids were speeding through my

1. National Institute on Drug Abuse, *Anabolic Steroids*.

The Lecture

father's veins full throttle, and in addition to being verbally aggressive (thank you, steroid researchers), he started to be physically abusive toward my mother when caring for her. I had to yell at him to stop, pull him away, and made him stay apart from her for the remainder of the night. Of course, this meant I had to do the full evening routine on my own, from using the Hoyer Lift to fly her into bed, to getting her on the bedpan and changing her disposable underwear, to dressing her in her night clothes, to medicating her, and to finally sharing that ever-popular nightcap of wine and jellybeans.[2] And she was so hurt my father, who had rarely if ever raised his voice to her during almost fifty years of marriage, and was the kindest human on the planet, had treated her so horribly. I tried to explain the power of steroids, and how he was not in control of his behavior while under the influence of these powerful drugs, but hurt feelings are just hurt feelings. I sent my father to bed, instructing him only to sleep and not be a helper. I made sure my mother was as comfortable as a person can be when they cannot move their body on their own, and then I went upstairs to my kitchen and cried.

Between issues with the revolving door of home health aides and how my parents were treating one another, I had a lot on my heart and much to say. Really, friends, words and feelings were ricocheting in my brain like the small metal ball in a pinball machine. But getting my parents to welcome an impromptu conversation full of constructive criticism was not going to happen. So, in my infinite wisdom, I gave them a lecture the next day that I had written *in advance*, inspired of course by my parents' talent for

---

2. I could have asked my husband Paul to help me, but I desperately tried during those years of cohabitating with my parents *not* to involve him with personal or more intimate day-to-day caretaking. He was so generous and always willing to help with anything big picture, technical, or transportation related, but personal bedroom and bathroom care was all me. No matter how much the mother-in-law adores the son-in-law, and vice versa, some boundaries are healthy, and I tried desperately to defend those boundaries for both of their sakes. Sadly, sometimes those boundary lines occasionally blurred, and Paul graciously helped with personal matters when help was really needed. Since I was absent so much, Paul was also busy with maintaining our house and caring for our kids. We really had to divide and conquer doing those years.

interrupting and debating. I told them they could not speak until I was finished, and even then, I did not want debate, excuses, or explanations. I was giving them my observations to discuss amongst themselves.

The theme of the lecture was acknowledgement that, within their marriage, there were two people who were battling illnesses, and "while you may disagree with me, one of you is not more tormented than the other." I encouraged them to listen to one another more carefully (in addition to telling them it was time for my father to get a hearing aid and my mother to get an amplifier) and urged them to respect each other's requests knowing those requests came from places of raw vulnerability. I touched on better time management and their needing to embrace flexibility more enthusiastically, to let go of perfectionism, and how "good enough" is an acceptable standard. I demanded, in so many words, that they treat one another and caregivers with kindness and respect ("Being ill or disabled does not excuse you from being gracious and polite") and encouraged them to rely on their caregivers as much as possible for caregiving so they had more quality time with one another as husband and wife. Their sorrow for one another was equal, and they needed to be reminded that their illness experience was not a competition; they were equally yoked in every part of this journey (see Appendix C for the full lecture).

And they both listened, probably because despite my unintimidating five-foot-one-inch frame, I was draped in a bit of anger with a hint of bitter. And then I left them with a hard copy of my lecture so they could go back through word by word, line by line, and digest and debate it all they wanted. The tables had officially turned; I became the parent, and they became the children. I remember in explicit detail the handful of lectures I received from my parents when I was growing up when I had been especially naughty or had pushed the boundaries a little bit too far. And now I needed to lecture my parents because *they* were being especially naughty and pushing the boundaries too far! It felt good to get what I was thinking and feeling off my chest, but the transition from lecture recipient to the one doing the lecturing is a very

The Lecture

painful pit stop on the circle of life. It just does not feel right, even when we know the alternative is unacceptable, and potentially dangerous. My father shared with me that after the lecture, he and my mother did talk about all the points I had raised, and it did help in small ways with how they treated one another and others, but it did not change their attitudes about how much their situation supremely sucked. And why would it? I am, however, going to call the lecture a lukewarm win-win. Years later, I still stand by every emotion-filled point I raised with my parents that day. I think because my parents were in the thick of it so deeply, it was difficult for them to see the forest for the trees, and their getting someone else's perspective, even when they did not ask for it, was helpful. It was, at a minimum, helpful for me to share what was weighing so heavily on my heart. What did I learn from this lecture experience? That we do what we must do to keep the circle of life circling and eat Captain Crunch cereal only in moderation.

17
Possible Side Effects

As a child, did you ever eat alphabet soup? I rushed to see how many words I could spell on my spoon with the swollen pasta letters floating in hot steaming broth. I remember asking my mother for the big tablespoon so I could spell longer words, even though I could barely fit the spoon in my mouth. My strategy was consistent: actual words first, followed by new magical words I would create with leftover letters. I have a sneaking suspicion this is how drug companies brainstorm names for new drugs they have developed. I envision a board room full of men and women in white coats, PhD diplomas, bowls of alphabet soup, and the largest spoons they can find.

When my father was part of a clinical trial at the National Institutes of Health to treat his multiple myeloma, he was given a plethora of drugs, all with names I cannot easily pronounce: Lenalidomide, Carfilzomib, Omeprazole, Zolpidem, Ranitidine, Enoxaparin, Plerixafor, Filgrastim, Levofloxacin, Azithromycin, Pamidronate, ValACYClovir and more. Each prescription included a detailed list of possible side effects, which drug companies are legally obliged to include so consumers can make educated risk/benefit calculations. Sometimes, however, it feels like a dog and pony show. First, how sad our society needs to be instructed *not* to take the drug if we are allergic to it. Messaging to the lowest common denominator does not instill much confidence in the

Possible Side Effects

continuation of our species! I appreciate the importance of patients reporting side effects they experience, which is reasonable when there is only *one* drug. When there are over a dozen drugs and drug interactions, how on earth do the doctors expect us to keep this corollary data straight?

One drug my father ingested had over fifty possible side effects[1] alone, and I laughed out loud in disbelief when I read the list. I acknowledge this is serious business and people sadly die from negative side effects every day, but this list was over the top. The catalog of conditions included basics you would expect like fatigue, nausea, and headache, but also more obscure reactions like nosebleeds, double vision, and insomnia, and life-threatening realities including kidney, liver, and heart failure. It felt like, in an attempt to punk the patient, the drug maker considered every

---

1. So you can appreciate my exasperation, the list of possible side effects is listed here: Fatigue; Nausea; Anemia; Shortness of breath (at rest or with exertion), which in rare cases may be life-threatening or resulting in death; Upper respiratory tract infection; Thrombocytopenia: Decreased; Diarrhea; Mild decreases in renal function which are generally reversible; Vomiting; Fever; Headache; Constipation; Neutropenia; Swelling of arms or legs; Cough; Back pain; Loss or decrease in appetite which may lead to weight loss; Blood chemistry and electrolyte alterations; Pain, burning or irritation at the infusion site; Dizziness; Rash and/or Itching; Inflammation of the liver (mild, reversible changes in liver function tests); Pneumonia or other lower respiratory tract infections; Flu-like symptoms such as fever, chills, or shaking that may occur at any time; Insomnia (difficulty sleeping); Anxiety; Confusion or changes in mental state; Blurred or double vision; Numbness, tingling, or decreased sensation in hands and/or feet; Generalized pain; Pain in the bones or joint pain; Muscle spasm, pain, or weakness; General weakness, or lack of energy or strength; Abdominal pain, discomfort, or swelling; Indigestion (upset stomach); Increase or decrease in blood pressure; Urinary tract infection; Nosebleeds; Dehydration; Infusion reactions including flushing or feeling hot, fever, shakes, nausea, vomiting, weakness, shortness of breath, tightness in the chest, and low blood pressure; Inflammation of the pancreas (pancreatitis); Kidney failure which can lead to dialysis; Worsening liver function up to and including liver failure; Decreased or worsening heart function including chest pain, abnormal heart rhythm, heart attack and heart failure (may have a life-threatening or fatal outcome); Allergic reactions including total body rash, hives, and difficulty breathing; Blood clots in the legs or blood; Infections in the blood; Tumor lysis syndrome."

possible ailment the human body could experience and added it to *this* particular list.

A person has two options: not take the drug and die from cancer or take the drug but possibly die from any number of side effects. A real conundrum that would make even a professional Vegas gambler tremble in her shoes. With every pill, I noted behavioral and physical changes in my dad, recorded his personal observations and complaints, and prayed he would experience the fewest reactions possible, especially ones that could kill him. Ultimately, he sampled from a buffet of side effects: some bad, some manageable, some temporary, some permanent, but his cancer is now in remission. So, hats off to the alphabet soup doctors; I am
    T–R–U–L–Y   G–R–A–T–E–F–U–L.

18

Pills and People Who Listen

Around year two of three of my mother's illness, my tank was running on empty, being the daughter to sick parents and a mom to three children while also trying to fit in being a wife here and there. I used every bit of my energy to make life appear normal, but I slowly began to unravel. I was physically, emotionally, and spiritually spent, and no matter how hard I tried to spin, I could not morph into Wonder Woman. This was disappointing on many levels, but mostly because I desperately wanted to rock the blue and white star bottoms, red boots, and the corset that would undoubtedly lift and push my boobs up and make them look like they did before I nursed three children!

So short of being Wonder Woman, unravel I did. As I was driving home from dropping my children at school one morning, I experienced a full-blown panic attack. I had never had one, and it's fair to say, it scared the shit out of me. Torrential tears and not able to breathe, I had to pull over to the side of the road so I did not crash my car. My gratitude for cell phone technology and friendship was never greater. Through my hysteria, and with the help of low-powered radio frequency, my best friend Kristen gently and lovingly talked me down off the ledge, helped me find my breath, and we agreed it was time for me to talk with a professional. I experienced one more panic attack days later, conceded to needing help, made an appointment with my general practitioner, and started a prescription of anti-anxiety medication the same day. I am nothing if not efficient!

I am not a big pill taker. I will suffer through a headache instead of taking a single Advil, and I take childlike gummy vitamins daily. I have a very strong gag reflex and getting a pill down requires dramatic calisthenics as I throw my head back to open my throat, praying the pill slides down without my knowing. But I needed this medication. I was mourning the loss of my mother while she was still alive, struggling with the stress of caretaking, and the foreboding of a future I did not understand was taking its toll. I was scared. And the medication absolutely helped. It leveled me out enough so I could think more clearly, I panicked less frequently, and I did not cry every other moment.

But these feelings of raw vulnerability were not going anywhere, and I realized I needed some additional support. I called our church's Presbyterian reverend and asked him to please assign me a Stephen minister. Stephen ministers are lay congregation members (not clergy) trained to provide one-to-one care to those experiencing a difficult time in life. I kind of felt like I checked that box. I began meeting weekly with my Stephen minister who was caring, encouraging, and provided me emotional and spiritual support. She was a breath of fresh air, helping me at the worst time in my life by giving me a safe place to share what I was thinking and feeling. She was an amazing listener and conversationalist, and our shared faith and her forever friendship is a gift for which I will always be grateful.

After my mother passed away, I found my way to the clinical couch. I started weekly therapy sessions with a psychologist whose specialty was "grief," which matched up beautifully with my needs! And friends, I learned there is *nothing* easy about therapy. I saw my therapist every week for two years, unpacking all I had experienced for the three years before my mother passed away. Therapy forced me to be honest and talk about experiences and feelings I had only barely vocalized to another human. I entertained all the emotions possible on that clinical couch—sorrow, anger, humility, frustration, fear, embarrassment, shame, disgust, nostalgia, and eventually, I was able to experience more joy, optimism, and relief. Therapy did that. Therapy gave me fifty minutes to cry so I could sing in the choir on Christmas Eve service and make it through in one piece. Therapy gave me the courage to talk with my dad about moving out of our house a year and a half after my mom passed away and starting anew. Therapy gave me the freedom to be a devoted mother, loving wife, and good friend to other people again. Therapy gave me the courage to write about all I had experienced in caring for my mother, hoping it might help just one other person on planet Earth. When I "graduated" from therapy two years after my mother passed away, I remember leaving the office building with a little more pep in my step and thinking about just how beneficial therapy had been for me and how I wished every caregiver could benefit from the luxury of the clinical couch.

What I learned more than anything through panic attacks, side-of-the-road phone calls, pills, Stephen ministers, and time on the clinical couch is it's okay to ask for help. While you may be feeling weak, asking for help is not a sign of weakness. It was humbling for sure when I realized I was not invincible, because damn, I thought I was! But I don't think as humans we are expected to go through life's struggles alone. If anything, we are genetically programmed to help one another and build each other up when things go south. "We're wired to be other regarding. We shrivel if there is no other . . . evolutionary science has come to see cooperation, and its core emotions of empathy, compassion, and generosity, as fundamental to our species' survival."[1] According to the smart scientists, asking for help means our species will survive. Here's my two cents (really, that is all my advice is worth): if talking with a professional seems too intimidating, start small and talk with a friend, the random person you meet while riding the bus, or the sweet guy who collects the grocery carts in the supermarket parking lot (Joe and I have great conversations many times a week!). Really, humans love to talk with other humans, so just reach out. But I encourage you to feel confident in reaching out to a professional too—a doctor, therapist, clergy person, or hotline;

1. Dalai Lama, et al., *Book of Joy*, 257–58.

these wonderful people are very well trained, and they did not let me down. I know my asking for help meant I could continue living, loving, and showing gratitude for every day. And while I have not completely abandoned my hope to one day rock the red, white, and blue Wonder Woman uniform, I learned in the short term that asking others for help was the best way to survive.

19

Walking Her Home
A Love Story

MUSIC HAS A WAY of touching our souls and releasing emotions our very intellectual minds keep buried, or at least keep generally in check. Sometimes we can hear just the first few notes or chords of a song, our eyes well up at a minimum, and at full throttle, the tears really start flowing. We have not even gotten to the lyrics, but we know what's coming, and our soul knows as well. These are songs that spoke to us at moments in time when we needed to hear their message. And they stick with us, like peanut butter and marshmallow fluff to Wonder Bread, and bring us back to those poignant moments in our lives whenever we hear the tune and lyrics again. These are the songs that cause us to pull over because we can't see through the tears when we are driving.

I had the privilege of witnessing a real-life love affair even more powerful than the best romantic film or classic novel. I always knew my parents loved one another. I always knew they enjoyed each other's company over the company of any other person. When I was little and they flirted, I would throw myself in between them wanting to be part of the fun, and when I was old enough to understand what flirting was, I would giggle from a distance. My parents loved being together and each made the other a better person. My father challenged my mother to find joy and spontaneity

Scratch My Itch

in life and my mother reigned my father in. Each was the yin to the other's yang. They loved dancing, working, relaxing, and planning together; a work hard, play hard couple, they were both equal in the work and play. That is not to say they did not argue, or quibble, or get frustrated or impatient with one another. They were not a superhuman love affair after all. They were just what all of us hope and pray we find during our lifetimes—a partner who is a trusted confidante, cheerleader, motivational speaker, lover, partner in crime, advocate, coworker, and friend. And someone who will walk you home.

I don't remember when I heard this song for the first time or who led me to it when my mother was ill, but there it was: Mark Schultz's song "Walking Her Home." This song spoke to me and captured the essence of my parents' relationship: they dated and got married, they adventured through life together, and then my father walked my mother home. I remember one night quite a bit into my mother's illness, when my mom and dad were flirting with each other, still so in love after fifty plus years, despite the horrors, sorrow, annoyances, and frustrations of a terminal illness. I came upstairs after caring for them and typed a note to my best girlfriends: "Tonight, my mom and dad were flirting with each other and so in love, despite it all." Isn't that true love?

My father is a saint. To quote the hymn "I Sing a Song of the Saints of God," saints "lived not only in ages past, there are hundreds of thousands still . . . you can meet them in school, or in lanes, or at sea, in church, or in trains, or in shops, or at tea."[1] My father, the modern-day saint, was by my mother's side from start to finish. He showed up. He did the hard stuff husbands and wives should not have to do for the other, but they do. He made sure she was fully cared for, loved, celebrated, and cherished. Which is why I was so moved when she was so far into her illness, and so incapacitated, and I found them flirting like school kids. What a gift for them, and what a gift I got to witness and keep.

---

1. The hymn "I Sing a Song of the Saints of God" was written in 1929 by Lesbia Scott and is sung to the tune of *Grand Isle* composed by John Henry Hopkins in 1940 and is Hymn 364 in *The Presbyterian Hymnal*.

Walking Her Home

My father slept next to my mother during her entire illness. Not once did he ever consider she sleep independently from him or he from her. This, of course, meant he was up constantly during the night, helping to readjust her body, respond to any need, and for the entire time she was ill, he never got a full night of sleep. I am 100 percent confident my father never thought there was ever an option of *not* being with my mother in this way. When they got married and wore hand-braided crowns of self-sacrifice, from that moment on they happily accepted what was required of them in marriage. When equally yoked, each carries the burdens of the other, during the day and during the night.

Mark Schultz's song "Walking Her Home" is this song for me, that when I hear it on the car radio, I cannot see through my tears. It has been ten years since my mother passed away, and the tears are no fewer than when I heard it the first time. As soon as I hear the opening A–G–A note sequence and the words "lookin' back," I know I need to pull over. And I will usually cry through the song, then pause to catch my breath, and finally give thanks. Gratitude for the love affair my parents experienced together, gratitude for the love affair I got to witness as their daughter, and gratitude my father was there to walk my mother home.

"Walking Her Home" by Mark Schultz
Looking back
He sees it all
It was her first date the night he came to call

Her dad said son
Have her home on time
And promise me you'll never leave her side
He took her to a show in town
And he was ten feet off the ground

He was walking her home
And holding her hand
Oh, the way she smiled it stole the breath right out of him
Down that old road
With the stars up above

Scratch My Itch

He remembers where he was the night he fell in love
He was walking her home

Ten more years and a waiting room
At half past one
And the doctor said come in and meet your son

His knees went weak
When he saw his wife
She was smiling as she said he's got your eyes
And as she slept, he held her tight
His mind went back to that first night

He walked her through the best days of her life
Sixty years together and he never left her side

A nursing home
At eighty-five
And the doctor said it could be her last night
And the nurse said Oh
Should we tell him now
Or should he wait until the morning to find out

When they checked her room that night
He was laying by her side

Oh he was walking her home
And holding her hand
Oh the way she smiled when he said this is not the end
And just for a while they were eighteen
And she was still more beautiful to him than anything
He was walking her home
He was walking her home

Looking back
He sees it all
It was her first date the night he came to call

Walking Her Home

"He walked her through the best days of her life . . ."

20

Unpacking

WHEN A PERSON IS given a diagnosis that offers no hope, and that person understands there are limited days remaining in their time on earth, there is a lot of unpacking that starts to happen, for the person dying and for the people who love them. There is unpacking of the physical stuff we accumulate over the course of our lives—and all the emotional stuff. This process of unpacking is similar to when a pregnant woman reaches the last trimester and starts frantically nesting to prepare for the arrival of her baby, but the end for which we are preparing is death.

It is a curious thing when you pack up the house of a married couple who are parents to two adult children, all of whom don't like to throw things away, and who kept everything for "memory's sake." And it's an even more curious experience when that character trait (really, let's just call it what it is: a very bad habit) spans three generations. Simply put, it translates to a lot of crap! And we got to move it *all* from New Jersey to Maryland. Much of it came to our new house that we all now shared. And a significant amount went to two large storage units one town over. These storage units were packed floor to ceiling with furniture and boxes filled with treasures from not only my childhood and my parents' lifetimes, but also my grandparents' and great grandparents' possessions that my mother never had the stomach or time to clean out. My mother was sick for two years in our new home, and you would think that would have been plenty of time to unload the storage units. Nope. See that requires time, of which we had none because of caregiving, *but* it also requires a consensus that it is okay to get rid of things. My mother did not want to part with anything. Not the forty or so pieces of framed artwork she had collected over a lifetime, some of which she didn't even like; the bed sheets for beds she no longer owned; or even the "garage sale find" B. Kliban black-and-white-striped cat with red sneakers ceramic bank! She was sure she would eventually unpack every box and find a place for all these things in the six hundred square feet of space that was her new home.

What I realized as she became increasingly incapacitated and closer to dying, is *I* had some unpacking to do—and not just of my mother's moving box empire. As my mother's illness progressed, I felt this overwhelming need to share with her just how incredible a mother she had been to me. I grew up in a family where we say "thank you" and "I love you" *all* the time. We say "thank you" for every little thing from making the bed, to holding a door, to cooking a nice dinner, to hosting a baby shower, to complimenting you on your ugliest day. And "I love you" at the end of every phone call; when we leave each other for work, school, or errands; and at bed every night. If you grew up in our family, there was no question you were appreciated for anything nice you did and just how much you were loved. But there are all those other thoughts of gratitude, appreciation, and love we think about, and reflect upon, as we become adults and look back at our childhoods but have not yet verbalized. And while we can have these moments of revelation during happy times in our life, there is nothing like a death sentence to make you want to share all that is in your heart with the person who is dying.

But where to start, oh, where to begin? Hallmark, of course! They published a book of prompts titled *Mom*, and wouldn't you know, it was the perfect tool to get my juices flowing, and it gave me the opportunity to write and share with my mother my favorite memories and formally thank her for being my incredible mother. I shared my earliest memories about the feel of the linoleum, brown-tiled floor in the kitchen of our family's first home, the chartreuse shag carpet in my bedroom, the dirty sandbox in the back yard, and the freedom I felt in each of those spaces. I recalled the time my mother asked me to wash up before bed and the time she caught me in a lie when she realized the soap and washcloth were not wet, and I formally apologized. I let her know I always found her walk-in closet to be a magical place, and I disclosed the secret discoveries I had made while snooping in there, like letters she and my dad wrote to one another when he was away in Vietnam or the trashy novel I found (and how I read all the steamy parts and learned a lot quickly in just one day!). I shared how much I loved spending time with her at our local Avon beach and the joy of a canister of Pringles on beach days. I made sure she knew just how much I loved looking through pattern books with her and picking out perfect fabrics for clothes she was going to make my sister and me, like the peach terry cloth shorts jumper, or my eighth grade graduation dress made of pink Dotted Swiss. I shared hundreds of memories about how she made me feel safe, things I wish I had done differently, times when I was wrong and she was definitely right, her best advice I have cherished, my favorite meals she cooked, how she and I are most similar and how we are most different from one another, favorite gifts received, funny stories, ways she tried to keep me out of trouble, memorable trips, her superpowers, and her endearing quirks.

Of course, the prompts do raise personal questions, and you are left to decide whether you should really be sharing the honest answer with your mother on her deathbed. I had written one response to the prompt "Tough Love Can Be Tough" and then proceeded to erase it. Never put it in the book and she never read it. The response was about the first time I had sex, which I was not supposed to do until I was married . . . but I did.

> Well, I don't know how you did it, but you brainwashed me all through childhood about all sorts of things! In my preteen years, I remember "no makeup" and then "a little makeup" and then "woah, Cyndy, too much makeup!" You taught me how to do it right. Oh, and "no high heels"

Unpacking

when everyone else started wearing them. I remember our going to Pappagallo for narrow *flat* shoes. And well, somewhere along the way, you taught me that sex before marriage was bad. You made me think there would be flames if I had sex before marriage! Without confessing anything, there were *no* flames, and I was awfully confused.

Truth be told, I lost my virginity, and the first words out of my mouth were, "Where are the flames?" You can imagine the confusion on my poor boyfriend's face!

What did I learn from this experience? Unpack what needs unpacking. Share what is in your heart that will build the other person up. Share your favorite memories, or if truly necessary, share things that have been weighing heavily on you. But you have the freedom and prerogative to choose *not* to share something. That is okay, too.

The person who is dying has emotional unpacking to do as well—sharing critical advice and reminiscing over favorite family adventures and the happy moments in life. But there is also a need to unpack secrets, demons, and disappointments that have burdened a person during their lifetime. I find there are many facts kids intrinsically know about their parents; we may not remember how or when we learned these facts or stories, but through osmosis of growing up with our parents, and I assume hearing stories repeated, we do. In our family, for example, it was inherent knowledge that my dad, who was one of eight children of an immigrant family, worked from a young age to contribute to the family income. As a teenager he used to drive an ice cream truck, and he also worked every day after school in the family's dry-cleaning store (and was able to keep any spare change he found in the pockets of the clothes he was cleaning!). In my mother's case, her adventure stories, which centered mostly around her growing up in the Ukrainian Orthodox Church, were common knowledge, and we inherently understood and appreciated where she came from and why her ethnicity was important to her. But there are also many things we don't know about our parents, things they never thought to share or chose not to share.

Scratch My Itch

    One day, toward the end of her illness, my mother asked me if I wanted to know why she was always so private, why she did not share thoughts and feelings with other people very easily. This was a woman who protected her privacy so much she didn't even want to tell people she had a terminal disease. Keep in mind, this was one of her character traits that used to drive me bananas and she knew it. I am an open book! I will tell you anything and share the most personal stories with perfect strangers. But I also had not been abused. This was the secret my mother shared with me as she laid literally, on the bed on which she would die just weeks later. There was a man who lived in her strip of rowhouses who would sometimes take care of her when her parents were off at the factories working. And she was invited often to "sit on his lap" and all that implied. She said that except for my father, she had never told anyone. When I asked why she had not told her parents, she said it was because she knew her father would have killed the man. I imagine it was beyond hard, unfathomable to me, to carry that secret for a lifetime. And processing that experience as a child, and then as a young woman, and then as an adult, and trying to live a healthy life without ever having unpacked trauma like that. My heart broke for my mother, the little girl whose innocence had been taken away and who must have been so scared and confused and hurt, and for my mother, the sixty-nine-year-old ALS victim, who felt it was information that needed to be shared finally with her daughter, lest she not have another opportunity to do so.

    Finally, there is the unpacking that happens after your beloved person dies. Sending favorite clothing items to friends who wear the same size and donating clothes to people who will never know the story behind the shirt or sweater they put on. Selling the mother-of-the-bride dresses worn on my wedding day and my sister's wedding day. Unpacking boxes of photos, slides, and reel-to-reel videos that over a lifetime were never sorted or cataloged or put into albums. Figuring out what to do with the pack of love letters, tied with a tattered piece of string, written between my grandparents from when they were courting and one lived in Woonsocket, Rhode Island, and one lived in South Boston,

Unpacking

Massachusetts, and there were no telephones. Common household items, valuable personal effects, and cherished mementos all need to be unpacked and managed, and this process is part of the amazing circle of life.

My takeaway from this experience is unpacking the physical and the emotional is much like the Wildcat wooden roller coaster at Hershey Park in Pennsylvania. It has its highs, and it has its lows; really, you are barreling over hills, bumps, and turns at forty-five miles per hour in a small car on wooden tracks. It is time consuming, gut wrenching, and simultaneously mind-numbing and fascinating. It reveals things and it helps tidy things up. And unpacking is absolutely, positively necessary.

> Oh my, opening the box of your mother's things made her seem so close and yet, at the same time, also makes it so real that she is not with us. Thank you so, so much for including me in the people who received some of her things. I will feel she is a part of me when I wear them. The sweaters are lovely (I've never had a holiday sweater—that will be fun!), and the shoes and boots are all wonderful. She was a classy woman!
> —Email from a family member.

21

Eulogyland

THERE WERE SO MANY days and nights when the majority of my time was spent caring for my mother, surrounded by the less than beautiful landscape of medical equipment and the necessities of daily care including bed pans, bed liners, disposable underwear, medicines, and supplements. My mother was not fun to be with, and I was not winning any humanitarian awards; at this point I was just going through the motions hoping to survive. And there was just so much clutter. In addition to everything medical, my parents tried to fit as much as they could of their large five bedroom, two and a half bath house into two rooms in our new home. Clutter everywhere. And clutter makes me all sorts of crazy! So, every night my internal coping mechanism would kick in, and I would look around the room and item by item, dispose of it in my mind. *Every night*, I would subconsciously unpack those two rooms—what was to be saved and cherished, what was to be given away to family or friends, what would be donated, and what would go to our local dump. Item by item. I was internalizing Marie Kondo and was loving and celebrating the magic I found in tidying up.

    I also started planning my mother's funeral, which may sound inappropriate and premature to you. It seemed that way to me. At the time, I felt guilty for having these thoughts and doing this pre-planning. And even today, there is a part of me that still feels guilty for having spent time burying her in my mind before she had passed. Did I waste time focusing on death instead of celebrating life? Absolutely. I did not want my mother's life to end, and I could not imagine my life without her. But there were nights when I hoped it would all end because caregiving was exhausting and futile. The challenge with ALS is there is no cure, and thus, there is no hope. It just was, and it would only get worse. We all know how the story ends. So, in addition to funeral planning,[1] I started writing her eulogy. There were nights when I would finish caring for my mom long after midnight but needed to unwind before I could lay my head on the pillow and fall asleep. I would pour myself a glass of wine (or two . . . or three), sit at my computer, and write. I wrote her eulogy long before she had taken her last breath. Not only had I written it, but I had spent hours editing it. And had practiced saying it, half out loud. Welcome to Eulogyland, my friends!

Eulogyland, like Disneyland, implies fun. But when I say "eulogies," "are," and "fun," in that order, I find I rehearse the phrase repeatedly in my head and out loud trying to find the right inflection for the statement. Is it an excessively punctuated positive exclamation about the amazing opportunity we have to share with the world what an incredible person our family member or friend was, funny stories that make us laugh, and testimony that comforts us and inspires us? Eulogy, by definition, implies happy since it is "a speech or piece of writing that praises someone highly."[2] Reminiscing happy, funny, and tender memories *is* fun.

Or is "Eulogies are fun?" a question, with sarcastic tenor, because who in their right mind would ever even think to make that statement? I love writing, but writing when you are grieving makes putting the words on the paper a little *less* fun. And while praising the person you have loved and lost is a beautiful moment, I would not rush to call it fun, because again, grief. *Or* is "Eulogies are fun" a matter-of-fact statement, said with just enough confidence to

---

1. I spent time thinking about all the details I would need to manage once my mother did pass away. I have a short list of anticipated funeral action items I have since shared with many friends and I have included it at the end of this book in case it could ever be helpful to you (see Appendix B).

2. Oxford Languages, *Oxford Dictionaries Online*.

draw the other person in for a more detailed explanation about the practical nature and purpose of this long-held tradition of paying homage to a person who has passed away? The word "eulogy" derives from the Greek word *eulogia*, and it was first documented in the fifteenth century. So, fun fact, we've been writing eulogies for quite some time, approximately 622 years! History is fascinating, isn't it?

Back in the late 1990s and early 2000s, I spent a lot of time writing my dissertation as one of the many requirements to earn my PhD in Criminal Justice. The number of hours I spent writing this research tome was exponential, and it is mind-numbing now to think about how difficult and challenging it was to write all 181 pages. And writing a dissertation has nothing on writing a eulogy! With a eulogy, in a short amount of time (ballpark, ten minutes or less), you need to say everything that needs saying about the person who died. You need to summarize their life (which when they are old takes even longer), note their accomplishments, praise their special qualities, and acknowledge their loved ones who have come before and those who are still alive and mourning. The eulogy needs to be respectful and solemn but peppered with humor, hope, and comfort. It shares special stories, and it celebrates the life of the person who has died. So much pressure on one little exposition! And the room full of people listening to the eulogy are judging; not intentionally and not to be mean, but they are simply waiting to see what you do with the opportunity. Did you include all the things they would have included? Did you balance the right amount of pithy with humor? What revelation did you share they did not know? Did you make it through without crying, or did someone have to step in and deliver the eulogy for you because you could not keep it together? Is the person delivering the eulogy going to be in the fetal position for the next few months, or is there a glimmer of hope when they talk that gives us enough confidence, they will be able to stand upright and ultimately be fine?

Tough to write and difficult to deliver, but what a blessing and privilege it is to be able to reflect on a person's life and celebrate all that made them special. We do this sometimes at milestone

Eulogyland

birthdays, retirement parties, and weddings in short speeches or toasts before we clink a glass. And the person hears the beautiful words people are sharing about them. But it is only at funerals where we really pull out all the stops and gush on people. And maybe it's because they are not there to blush that we feel we can go all out and spare not a single important sentiment. Maybe eulogies serve the purpose of not just celebrating the person who has passed but of giving the eulogy writer the first opportunity to step forward into the new life that does not include the person who died. Maybe the eulogy is the first step toward healing.

Looking back, while it did feel premature to write my mother's eulogy while she was still alive, it was helpful to write at my leisure; to write, let the words sit for a few days, and come back to them with fresh eyes; to have time to remember those thoughts that simmer in our unconscious when we are drifting off to sleep or waking up; to lovingly think about all of my mother's wonderful qualities instead of focusing on the person she had become as she struggled to survive. It was helpful that we needed to only make a few additions and edits to the premature eulogy after she passed away, rather than having to quickly write it from scratch while taking care of all the other funeral arrangements and while we were in a fog of sadness. In hindsight, writing the eulogy in advance took some of the pressure off!

My sister and I delivered the eulogy at my mother's service (see Appendix D to read the eulogy). We each took turns speaking, which gave us moments to collect ourselves before having to speak again, which was a very smart strategic move. We hope we did our mother proud with what we said and how we said it. I hope more than anything though that my children will one day reread it and remember how incredible their grandmother was. Then I will feel the eulogy best served its purpose.

This is where I come out on the inflection question. There is absolutely an exclamation point after the words "Eulogies are fun!" and also a period and definitely a question mark. Similar to how my children paste multiple emojis at the end of a text, I almost feel like we need to punctuate the hell out of the phrase "Eulogies are

Scratch My Itch

fun!?.!?.!?." to capture how we all really feel. That seems like the fair and faithful thing to do.

> I remember how neat your house in Lincroft was, and how when I came over, there was always a craft or some kind of activity for us to do. In Mendham, I remember taking recorder lessons from your mom. I have never learned to play another instrument. Oddly, with all the moves over the years, I still have that recorder and I can still play a few tunes on it. When I'm going for a high note, I can remember your mom adjusting my fingers to cover only half the hole. I remember her teaching me and my sisters and mother how to draw and dye Ukrainian Easter eggs. Mom still has the stylus with the red handle. I know my egg was ugly, but I thought it was beautiful and your mom was very complimentary . . . I think your mother could have had a great *paklava* business, wow it was yummy.
> —Email from a childhood friend after my mother passed away

> I had great respect for Barbara, for her dedication and commitment to her students, for her kindness, her intelligence, her maturity. I remember her always baking a birthday cake each year for a student who normally would not get one. I trusted her and her integrity.
> —Email from a fellow teacher after my mother passed away

> Barbara Nahabedian wasn't just a teacher; she was an angel sent from heaven. As a teacher she was able to see the possibilities in her students and pull them out. She was there for my son and helped him in ways I will always be thankful for.
> —Email from a parent of a student my mother taught sent after my mother passed away

You have been a most devoted and loyal employee of ECLC of New Jersey (Education, Careers, and Lifelong Community) for fifteen years. Most importantly, you are considered to be one of the finest teachers to ever have worked at ECLC in our forty-year history. Parents of

Eulogyland

students who passed through your classroom portal still speak your name with great affection and appreciation. In my forty plus year career, I have never seen anyone work harder or accomplish more. You have reached children who most deemed unreachable. You have given your all as well as taken inordinate amounts of time from your family life to ensure that you did the best for your students every day. You never took one lesson lightly! You always worked the 'night shift' at ECLC . . . I will miss my once or twice a year observation of you working your magic. No one does it better.
—Excerpt from a letter the executive director sent to my mother at the time of her retirement. This letter was read in full at her memorial service.

22

Ode to the Commode

MY MOTHER LOVED ACCESSORIES! She was the woman who matched her belt to her shoes and coordinated jewelry with every outfit she wore. She had scarves and gloves that went with different winter coats that also matched the clothes she was wearing. She had purses for every season and every outfit. She was *that* woman. Sorting through her accessories after she passed away was a huge job but was also fun in many ways. A real treasure hunt! Accessories from the 1950s, 1960s, and 1970s are considered vintage and are totally chic again. I am waiting for the opportunity to wear the elbow length white gloves, the fox stole, the metal coin belt, and the blue crochet beanie I found—not all at the same time, of course.

But ALS brings an entirely new set of accessories. All sorts of equipment—grab bars, ramps, commodes, shower chairs, a comb with a long handle, raised toilet seats, bed rails, transfer bench, wheelchairs, oxygen machine, Hoyer Lift, suction machine, pinchers to get things that are too high to reach, not to mention the adult disposable underwear (*never* use the word "diaper"), the disposable bed pads, and the feeding tube equipment. The list feels endless. And really, these accessories take on a life of their own, and they become an integral part of the landscape within your home. They are reached for affectionately because we all know life without these accessories would be that much worse. But these accessories also add a great deal of clutter. And if you are a person who does not like clutter, well then, life with all the accessories becomes a living hell.

It takes courage to confess there were many days or late evenings, when the hours of caretaking were just eating at my very soul, and I would look around my mother's bedroom at all the ALS-associated clutter and I would think, "I will be able to get rid of all of this one day" and it made me feel . . . *good*! Yup, good. That is my confession. But after I enjoyed those few moments of feeling good, I would then feel guilty for being so shallow as to wish for the day when all the medical clutter was not staring me square in the face because the only reason the medical clutter would not be there is because my mother would have passed away. And this was a thought I could not bear.

But then she died. And literally, the *minute* after the men from the funeral home came to take her body, I went into crazy clean up mode. Like "Martha Stewart on steroids" crazy cleanup mode. I took a trash bag and started dumping. I disposed of bed sheets and tubing, pads and medicines, feeding tube accessories and half-used water bottles. And then I could not stop. I went to her vanity, and I dumped her toothbrush, makeup and mascara, and half-used tubes of potions and lotions. I started gathering the larger pieces of equipment—the Hoyer Lift, the power chair, the breathing machine, the computer that was supposed to help her communicate that she never used, and I piled it all in the corner of another room. It was as if I had to accomplish all I had been thinking about for the past two years in a half hour or less. I had to get it out of my house. And it had to be now.

But let me back up for a minute. The morning my mother passed away my father had an appointment at the National Institutes of Health (NIH) for his own day of medical treatment as part of the clinical trial for his multiple myeloma. His participation that day was mandatory, and I don't think it ever dawned on any of us he *not* go, just because my mother had passed away that morning. So, my dad left for NIH just shortly after we found my mother had passed (like within an hour, folks), and I was left with my mother. She was dead. And I waited for the hospice nurse to come and declare she was indeed deceased. And then I waited for the funeral parlor people to come and take her away. And all I kept thinking about was my dad. He was sitting by himself receiving cancer treatment having just lost the love of his life, and he was going to come home to a room he shared with my mom, and all I could think about was how I wanted to clean it as quickly as possible of all things horrible.

To this day, I am not sure what his reaction was upon coming home and finding everything cleared out. As if Mom had never been sick in this space. I know for the week after she passed away, he slept upstairs in our guest bedroom and not in the bedroom he had shared with my mom. And I know we very quickly ordered a new mattress for his bed to be delivered to our house. Despite my efforts to take away the horrible—the equipment, the medical supplies, the medicines and supplements, the bedpans and feeding tubes—and make his space as livable as possible, it was still a space without my mother. No matter how much I tried, I don't think my father ever considered that space "home" again. Home was where my mother was, and she was not there.[1]

---

1. Before sending my final manuscript off to Wipf and Stock Publishers, I asked my father if he would please read my story before I shared it with the rest of the world. He thankfully gave me his blessing for printing all that you are presently reading. He also made a handful of notes in the margins as he read. Next to the sentence "To this day, I am not sure what his reaction was upon coming home and finding everything cleared out" he wrote, "surprised and pleased." I am so happy to now know how he felt about the results of my "Martha Stewart on steroids" moment and am so grateful his reaction was as positive as possible on a day our hearts were truly broken.

23

Mad Kitchen Skills, Persuasive Essays, and the Rock of Gibraltar

> [My mother's illness] has challenged my faith like never before and it's been really hard for me. At one point recently, I broke down and the only word I could get out was "please". I am hoping God could read what was in my heart. I am also worried about our kids, who will see her get worse and worse, in their home. But I hope they will have some special time together until we get to that point.
>
> —Email I sent to a friend

It is a beautiful Saturday morning, the sun is streaming through the kitchen windows, and my oldest daughter Alexandra, eleven years old at the time, saunters into the kitchen, sits down at the table, pulls a place mat in front of her, and waits. My son Matthew, age nine, follows soon after; he too sits down at the kitchen table, pulls a place mat in front of him, puts his water bottle on it, and waits. Eventually, our youngest, five-year old Juliette, dances into the kitchen straight to the refrigerator. She pulls a carton of orange juice from the top shelf, barely reaching it, and selects a plastic clamshell with strawberries and a container of yogurt from the middle shelf. She grabs a small step stool and opens the upper kitchen cabinet reaching to get a bowl. She pulls a cutting board and a plastic cup from the lower cabinet and a knife and spoon from the kitchen drawer. She proceeds to spoon herself some yogurt, cut some strawberries, pour a glass of orange juice, and carry each to the kitchen table, placing it all on her place mat with a napkin she has gracefully laid at her side. Our five-year old chef sits down to a wonderful breakfast with her older siblings jealously looking on as they wait for their food to magically appear.

Occasionally, I am asked what it was like for my children to live with a grandparent who had a terminal illness. Was it just horrible for them? Were they sad all the time? How scared were they? Are they haunted forever knowing their grandmother passed away in their home? These are fair questions. And the honest response is that each of them responded to our family situation differently. Their experience was dependent in part on their developmental age, their personality, and the relationship they had with my parents. I can say with confidence that despite this time of household stress and turbulence, there were, over time, silver linings that emerged for each of my children.

Juliette was just three years old when my parents moved into our collective new home and I started helping with my mother's caretaking. Juliette was your typical happy and carefree preschooler, focused on running, playing, dancing, and her voracious appetite, and I am not sure she understood much about our new stressful family situation. In her mind's eye, there were two more people in the house who loved her, and the more the merrier! I did my best to balance taking care of my mother and my children, but if I am being honest, my kids often got the short end of the stick. It was not unusual for me to go down to the basement to help my mother with a task I thought would take a few minutes, only for it to snowball into greater and longer caregiving, and I would finally climb the stairs back to my children a couple of hours later. What this meant is that Juliette learned to fend for herself at a *very* young age. Mom was too busy to get her a snack, so she learned to help herself to the pantry and refrigerator. Mom was too busy to get her dressed, so she picked out her own creative outfits. Mom was too busy to play with her, so she made her own fun. To this day, Juliette is the most resilient and independent young girl, still happy and carefree, rarely asking for help, figuring things out on her own, which is what she had to do for two years while I was dividing my time between my parents and the rest of the family. Independence and mad cooking skills are Juliette's silver linings.

When Matthew was in fourth grade, he had to write a persuasive essay for class. This assignment came soon after we moved from the home he was born into and loved to a new larger home one town over that would accommodate our family plus my parents. As he read his essay to the entire grade, including parents and teachers, all eyes turned to Paul and me to gauge our reaction, and then they turned with compassionate glances back to our son. Matthew's self-selected persuasive essay topic was "neighborhood design," and he eloquently articulated why he thought houses should be built closer together, like our old house, rather than farther apart, like our new house. Matthew argued that a neighborhood design where houses are closer together provides friends with whom to play, neighbors who can help in times of trouble, and people from whom you can borrow a cup of sugar or a toy. His final statement was "I have had the opportunity to live in both kinds of neighborhoods, and I prefer the smaller distance neighborhood." Stick a knife in me. I was done. We had uprooted our family to find a new home so we could care for my parents, and clearly, at least one member of our brood felt that trauma deeply.

Over time, in looking at Matthew's school writing, there were thankfully far more essays about the love he felt for his grandmother Babi and his grandfather Papa than disappointment over our family's new housing situation. Matthew continued to write in school about his experiences with my mother as she died and after she passed away, and I was grateful he had an outlet to share what he was feeling. He remembered how hard my mother tried to open her eyes when he came to kiss her good night the evening before she died and wrote, "My grandma and I had a very special connection. I was her first grandson, so I was the son she never had," which was both intuitive and correct! He also wrote about what he felt when he saw her after she passed away: "All the blood had drained out of the person that had calmed me down, held me as a baby, and played with me when I had nothing to do." In addition to nurturing Matthew's sensitivity, the experience of living with my parents while my mother was ill definitely fed Matthew's protective instincts; he was always looking out for and helping his grandparents and is still fiercely protective of my father today. My now college engineering student is always quick to open a door or help anyone who appears to need assistance, and he talks about one day becoming an architect. Strong protective instincts and, dare I say, possibly a career in neighborhood design are Matthew's silver linings!

Months before my mother passed away, we attended my husband's uncle's funeral in Canada. The family was clearly mourning his passing, but like any funeral, it was also nice having the extended family reunited and to see cousins, the next generation, playing happily together, a gentle balm for the sting of death. Following the funeral service, Alexandra, my oldest daughter, who is my rock, started crying and could not stop. Not a silent tear or a gentle weeping but gut-wrenching crying. I was so confused! She certainly knew Paul's uncle but not to that extent! She quickly shared she was not crying for Uncle Roupen, or for all the family who were feeling sad, but for Babi, her grandmother. Alexandra knew a funeral was coming, and she was overcome with sorrow. Hearing and seeing her little body sob were so difficult for me. We talked about how painful it is to accept that illness and death could ever be part of God's plan and that Uncle Roupen's funeral was unfortunately, or fortunately, our dress rehearsal. We cried over the reality that Babi's body was getting tired, and we would be going through this same type of ceremony sooner rather than later. It took my girl at least an hour to pull herself back together.

When my mother was diagnosed with ALS and my parents moved in with us, Alexandra was already nine years old. Two

Mad Kitchen Skills, Persuasive Essays, and the Rock of Gibraltar

years older than Matthew, and six years older than Juliette, she had logged the most time with my mother and father, and they were attached at the hip. Alexandra was my parents' first-ever grandchild, and my mother and Alex had a very special bond. Alexandra was old enough to understand what our family was doing and why we were doing it; she understood Babi was sick and was going to get worse, and we were going to get through it together and help as much as we could, because that is what family does. A performer and an equestrian, our perceptive and very practical girl was grateful her grandparents could now more often see her perform on stage or jump fences with her horses. Alex was old enough to appreciate how much work and sacrifice it took for my mother to get ready to come to see her in her activities, and she had nothing but gratitude for the extra time she was getting with her grandmother. Of our three children, Alexandra was our Rock of Gibraltar, and had a positive outlook with all that she did with my mother. Which explains why Uncle Roupen's dress rehearsal was so very painful for her. Alex's silver lining was more quality time with her grandmother and the appreciation that sometimes even a rock needs to crumble a little.

My children each have their own story to tell, and I hope one day they do share the details of what they remember. In short, I can say, living with my mother while she battled ALS was not horrible for my children and they were not sad all the time. If anything, quite the opposite! They loved this time with their grandparents, and despite caregiving, our house was full of fun and laughter. I am sure they were scared sometimes, just as I was scared when faced with something new concerning my mother's illness that I did not feel prepared for or did not understand. But we learned and then felt less scared. And unlike me, I do not think they ever thought their house was haunted because their grandmother passed away here!

I do think they learned valuable life lessons they could not have learned from a book or a lecture. I am grateful my children saw the immense love and self-sacrifice their grandfather showed their grandmother. My parents set an incredible example for my children of what is required of spouses in marriage, and I hope they will hold that example in their hearts forever and that it guides them in their life choices and relationships. I am grateful my children saw their grandmother show up to their school events, performances, karate belt tests, horse shows, church services, and more. It was like running a marathon every time we had to get my mother dressed and ready to go anywhere, but she was not going to miss being there to support her grandchildren. I know they had immense respect for my parents and the efforts they made on their behalf, and I pray they appreciate the value in just "showing up" as they go through life.[1] They absolutely developed greater compassion and sensitivity for people who struggle with disability, and I am proud when I see one of my children rush to open a door, pick something up, or help someone who is in any compromised condition. They anticipate needs beautifully now more than before and understand when help might be appreciated. They also saw the effort and sacrifice my husband made for his in-laws. We believe through marriage, we become one family, even if it means buying a new house and having your in-laws move in with you! Apologies to all you other husbands out there, but the Husband of the Year award goes to the love of my life Paul. He was the fairy godfather who graciously made this possible for our family.

We often hear inspirational and encouraging messages like "When life hands you lemons, you should make lemonade," "When God closes a door, somewhere he opens a window," and "Difficult roads often lead to beautiful destinations." But there is nothing like real life to make a person understand the value and perspective in statements like those. My hope is one day my children will be able to look back at the time they lived with their grandmother who battled ALS, and more quickly identify and celebrate silver linings the next time they face trial and tribulation. That would make my mother happy.

1. "Cyndy, I would like to thank your parents especially for coming to share in Grandparents' Day. I know there were challenges in getting to the classrooms, but their presence in the chapel and their sharing in the community event was well noted by your children and their teachers . . . Please thank your parents for their extraordinary effort to join us today."
—Email from a teacher at Christ Episcopal School, Rockville, Maryland

Mad Kitchen Skills, Persuasive Essays, and the Rock of Gibraltar

Miss Mad Kitchen Skills, Mr. Persuasive Essay, and Miss Rock of Gibraltar

24

Shakespeare-Inspired Conundrum

To ventilate or not to ventilate, that is the question! While maybe that is not the exact same question Hamlet raises in Shakespeare's play by the same name, the conundrum for an ALS patient of whether to live or not to live is absolutely the same. The word "ventilator" became part of the American vernacular during the COVID-19 pandemic, and we suddenly became a nation intimately familiar with how important ventilators are in supporting patients with compromised breathing. The person with ALS ultimately needs to decide if they want assistance in breathing when they can no longer breathe on their own. A raw, existential dilemma: Do they want to extend their life trapped within their body that can do very little on its own, except think and feel, *or* do they want to suffocate to death? Choosing between two evils, "To be or not to be?" is indeed the question.

Like characters in a Shakespeare drama, over our shared lifetimes, my mother and I had many meaningful, significant, challenging, and emotionally wrought conversations. But hands down, the hardest and most dramatic conversation I ever had with my mother was about end-of-life issues, specifically intubation and ventilation. For starters, neither of us wanted to have the conversation because the topic was scary, awkward, and was a blatant acknowledgement she was closer to dying. I knew, however, that avoiding the conversation would not make things easier for my mother, father, or me, in the short or long term. I asked about living wills, do not resuscitate (DNR) orders, and general policies and paperwork regarding their estate. My mother was devastated I even asked to have the conversation, and I felt like the absolute worst child on the planet. Her response to me was "My heart is already ten thousand times broken. How much more can I deal with? Everything has been taken away from me and I have nothing left. The end." But I assured myself someone needed to be the rational grown-up, and I reluctantly realized I was going to need the help of a professional if the conversation were ever going to happen. I again reached out to Anna, my new friend whose mother died of ALS and who went on to work for hospice. I needed a professional neutral party who could separate herself from the emotion of it all and speak from a place of intelligence, compassion, honesty, and experience. I asked Anna to be my Switzerland.

We gathered in my mother's bedroom: Anna, my father, my mother, and me, and as I anticipated, Anna professionally, compassionately, and honestly talked with my mother about her assorted end-of-life wishes including whether, when she could no longer breathe on her own, she wanted to be intubated and put on a ventilator. And with the bravado that comes with a compelling stage entrance, my mother said "*yes.*"

Yes? Did I hear her correctly? Yes? In an instant, a thousand thoughts flashed through my head and emotions exploded from my heart like a cheap Fourth of July firecracker. This was a woman who had talked about not wanting to live another day longer with this disease, could not move a single limb, could barely breathe, could not eat or do anything except think and feel, and she wanted to be put on machines to keep her breathing indefinitely. It is fair to say, I was shocked, angry, and upset about her decision, and I felt a little like how my father probably felt when he was jacked up on clinical-trial steroids—Captain Crunch crazy. That night, I replayed the conversation over and over in my mind and heard "*yes*" repeatedly, like a bell reverberates when being rung. What quality of life would that be for my mother, for my father, and for me? Yes, me. My mother's "yes" was her simple gut-wrenching confession that she was scared to die and did not want to leave us, and I had completely whitewashed her confession and was thinking about how her saying "yes" was going to affect . . . me. I was 100 percent confident I would not be able to handle taking care of my mother if she were intubated and attached to a ventilator, and my heart, while it could not imagine her dying and not being with me, could also not imagine seeing her hooked up to a machine indefinitely. I was scared and prayed she would ultimately change her mind.

    A short time later, my mother received her BiPAP machine, which is a non-invasive ventilation therapy that facilitates breathing. About the size of a toaster, the machine has a tube that connects to a mask that fits over a person's nose and mouth. The machine uses pressure to push air into the lungs, opening them up, thus improving the level of oxygen in the blood and decreasing the carbon dioxide. It is a game changer for the person who is beginning to struggle with their breathing in that it makes their breathing more comfortable and helps minimize the anxiety and panic that comes with not being able to inhale and exhale a full breath. And it's a stopgap measure until the person reaches that point when (and if) invasive intubation and a stronger ventilator is needed to keep the person breathing and alive.

    My mother tolerated a visit by Jane, one of the incredible staff at the ALS Association, who spoke with her about the nuts and bolts in using the BiPAP machine and also used the visit as an opportunity to talk with my mother about medication she would want to consider as she continued to experience changes in her breathing. Jane also spent some time talking with my mom about the pros and cons of intubation and ventilation. I was not there for this visit or discussion, but my father later recapped it for me in front of my mother, and I used it as an opportunity to share with them all I had been thinking, feeling, and praying about since my mother uttered the word "*yes.*" My father shared his thoughts too, as we took turns wiping tears from our own cheeks and my mother's cheeks. I acknowledged our collective fears. I reiterated

Shakespeare-Inspired Conundrum

how the process of intubation and ventilation was not going to be easy. We talked about the distinct possibility my mother would not be able to continue living at home if on a ventilator. I was honest when I told her I was not sure I could ever pull the plug on a machine that was keeping her alive if she were consciously looking at me. I shared how I thought it was more important for us to spend time focusing on her incredible life and all she experienced and accomplished and not have this disease define her. I told my mother I thought we needed to start praying for a different miracle: not a prayer to cure her disease but rather a prayer of gratitude for a life that had been filled with so much love.

My mother interrupted my horribly delivered monologue with two words: "*No tube.*" I choked on my words, sputtering to a stop, and stared at her in disbelief. I countered back, "No intubation or ventilator tube?" to which she shook her head in the affirmative and repeated, "*No tube.*" My eyes filled with tears and my heart was as conflicted and in pain as when I heard her say "*yes*" just a handful of days earlier. At some point between the conversation my mother had with Jane, and our honest sharing about feelings and fears later that same afternoon, she changed her mind and reversed her end-of-life instructions to her family.

We had all grown weary. It had been a long three years. And we could each argue our quality of life was less than stellar, my mother, of course, winning that prize. In uttering the words "*No tube,*" my mother acquiesced and surrendered, her white flag waving. From that moment on, we helped her be as comfortable as possible with the new BiPAP machine, learned what drugs needed to be administered at which moments in time, welcomed hospice into our home, spent as much time together as we could, and lived knowing at some point in the nearer than farther future, my mother would take her final curtain call. "To be or not to be" is indeed the question.

25

One Nurse, Two Nurse, Three Nurse, Four

AH, THE REVOLVING DOOR of home health aides! It's like a very bad version of the TV show *The Bachelor;* with each new aide, it's a bit like a first date, and there are first dates with many aides. And the likelihood that you find one who is your perfect fit, and with whom you might get a night in the Fantasy Suite, is pure fantasy folks. The challenge in our household was not entirely the quality of the aides, however, but the patient.

Just so we are perfectly clear, my mother did not want *any* home health aides in our home. She wanted only my father and me to care for her because that is comfortable. And I totally appreciated that. It is hard enough letting people you love and with whom you are comfortable assist you with very private orders of business—bathing, dressing, and toileting. It is a completely different ball of wax having people you don't know help you with those very private matters. Caregiving, however, is physical and mental gymnastics at the Olympic level, and when the person you are caring for requires someone to be at her beck and call 24/7 because that is the nature of her disease, home health aides are positively necessary if the *caregiver* wants to survive the disease. So, we convinced my mom we would bring in a caregiver to help during the weekdays, Monday through Friday, 9:00 a.m. to 5:00 p.m.—she would get the weekends off! And let's be honest. We didn't convince her; we told her how it was going to be. The gauntlet was thrown and the battle began: my mother versus every home health aide that walked through our doors.

We met so many wonderful, lovely, competent, compassionate, and hard-working home health aides. We also met some who only worked when being watched by a family member who was not my mother, who were rough in their caretaking, and who smuggled rolls of toilet paper home at the end of their shift. That is sadly the reality of home health aides. Like every other profession on the planet, it has good apples and bad apples. Getting to know each aide took time, and hours were spent teaching them what care my mother required and her preferences and dislikes. And building a rapport with your home health aide is a bit like building a sandcastle—bucket of wet sand on top of bucket of wet sand until eventually you make something that can sort of be construed as beautiful. But then my mother would be the giant wave that would wash it all away. She would be rude and insulting to the person who was caring for her, and the aide would not want to return. She would insist the person lacked all skills and credentials and demand someone else. She would be even more demanding than usual in hopes of wearing the person down.

I struggled desperately to reconcile the loving, gracious, polite, fun person who raised me and who I had known and loved my entire life with the woman who was prisoner to her bed and wheelchair and was rude to the people who were trying to help care for her. But I forgot to add "death sentence" to my equation when I did my calculations. She was so angry with this hand of cards she had been dealt, and as a result, she found being polite more than a little challenging. She was too bitter and uncomfortable to put the feelings of others before her own. I would get so embarrassed my mother was not being more gracious. But I also tried desperately to feel compassion for her as she was literally drowning in her own personal disease-infested waters. Her situation did not offer an end time she could look forward to, a disease expiration date that would be followed by health and wholeness. I imagine it is difficult to muster up the humanity to get through the dark period of strangers caring for you and literally wiping your ass if you know that this is what life is like until you go to meet your maker.

I can't say the home health aide story had a happy ending for my mother. She was never content with anyone we had helping us. But I do think she secretly appreciated and respected the one aide who worked with us the most, the longest, and until the end. Her name was Theresa, and she was to be revered in so many ways. She was competent and confident in her skills, respectful of my mother even when my mother was not being respectful in return, but she also knew how to occasionally put my mother back in her place. That superpower drove my mom crazy and equally comforted her. This was an aide who understood how to play both sides of the net.

But, thanks to Theresa, the home health aide story does have a happy ending in a slightly obscure way for me. As happens with ALS patients toward the end of their illness, my mother's breathing had become more difficult, she was experiencing feelings of air hunger which is the sensation of a strong urge to breathe or a feeling of severe breathlessness, and her energy levels had dropped tremendously. Even with the BiPAP machine, she was struggling and uncomfortable and panicking, rightly so, as she slowly suffocated. Both the ALS Association and Hospice explained to us that morphine, in appropriate doses, is very effective in relieving most of the symptoms of shortness of breath and air hunger and explained to us the physical reason why morphine works so well for these symptoms. Sparing you all the technical scientific medical jargon, morphine suppresses the body's drive to breathe when oxygen levels are low.[1] This wonder drug relieves the heavy breathing and shortness of breath challenges and diminishes the anxiety the person feels caused by feeling breathless. Ah-mazing.

---

1. "In the heart are receptors for the body to determine levels of oxygen reaching the heart muscles. If the levels are too low, the body is signaled to breathe more and harder to increase the levels of oxygen. Morphine has the property of dilating the coronary arteries, so that more blood reaches the receptors. More blood gives more oxygen, so the body signals that it's okay to relax now since the oxygen levels are better." ALS Association, *Living with ALS*, 10–11.

And morphine did what it was supposed to do for my mother. But this end-of-life wonder drug that equally generates fear and gratitude, also broke my heart. Crossing that medicinal threshold is the beginning of the end, and it's a conflicted path to tread.

We had put my mother to bed on a Tuesday at 11:00 p.m., almost two and a half years after she had moved in with us, and she slept the entire next day, waking only once or twice briefly—and only semiconsciously. Theresa thankfully continued to care for my mother as she always had during that daytime shift. My mother uttered a total of only six words to me that day: "wake me up" (which I tried to do and could not rouse her more), "meds," "help," and "morphine."[2] When I talked with her, she stared at me blankly as if she were someplace else. When my children came to kiss her good night, I could see her trying to open her eyes with all her might as she heard their little voices but she couldn't. As my husband and I tucked our children into bed that Wednesday night, I shared with them that Babi's body was getting tired, and while we didn't know when, her body would probably die at some point soon. There were true tears from my older children Alexandra and Matthew, and little Juliette, only five years old, went to bed asking two questions: "How does a person die?" and "Does it have germs?," a question I personally loved because clearly, she didn't understand what dying meant, or was thinking about how much she didn't want to catch what my mother had! My father and I got my mother ready for bed as we always did, but she slept the entire time, despite our moving her all over the bed. I kissed her good night, told her I loved her, and went to my bed upstairs. I said quiet prayers that my mother sleep with the angels and not suffer

---

2. My mother was fighting to live all the way to the end. When I think about her last six words, I crumble thinking about how scared she must have been. She wanted me to wake her up. She wanted me to help her. She didn't want to leave. But I also think she eventually realized she needed the morphine so she could die as comfortably as one can with ALS. My breath catches in my throat any time I hear the word "morphine." It is the last word my mother ever said to me and it's hard to shake that memory because I know she could not breathe. I respect the drug morphine for what it therapeutically provided my mother at the end of her life, despite its heartbreaking properties.

Scratch My Itch

and prayed for my father whose heart was breaking. I awoke with a start at 4:00 on Thursday morning, feeling like something was not right, but fell back asleep after convincing myself I must have had a bad dream. When I woke up a few hours later, I rolled out of bed still pajama-clad and walked immediately to the basement to check on my mother. I found my father still asleep by her side. I inched slowly toward her, touched her face, felt her cold body, and realized she had died. My heart dissolved into a thousand pieces as I went to wake my father.

That early morning, we were so wrapped up with our new sad reality of my mother's passing, I do not think it dawned on any of us that we should call the home health aide company to let them know. I am sure we would have gotten to that revelation eventually, but shock has a funny way of clouding human judgement. So, at 8:00 a.m. on the dot, Theresa showed up for her shift as usual. I sheepishly answered the door, profusely apologizing we had not yet called to let her know my mother had passed away during the night. She acted like I had just told her the sky is blue. She walked into my mother's room as she normally would greeting her "Good morning, Barbara!," peppy as all get out! I was seriously confused, friends. My mom is lying in bed deceased, and Theresa, as she always had, starts talking to my mother with all her usual morning pleasantries. And while she is talking to her, saying the nicest things, she walks over and closes my mother's gaping mouth, and pushes a pillow up under her chin to keep her mouth closed, letting me know if we did not do this now it would be harder to close her mouth later. She kept talking, the most wonderful elaborate one-sided conversation I had ever heard, and I stood there confused, as if I had possibly misread the signs. Was she still alive? Theresa then turned to me and, with the demeanor of a college professor, whispered, "Hearing is the last sense to go." Theresa, my mother's home health aide, who graciously weathered my mother's caustic attitude while doing yeomen's work, gave me a gift without even knowing it. She took control for a few minutes at the worst moment of my life and continued caring for my mother even when she did not have to. And in turn, she cared for me. She made me believe my mother could still hear what I wanted to say, which is "I love you. Please don't leave me."

26

Pink, Berry, Plum Maybe, but Never Peach

THERE ARE MANY THINGS for which we can prepare ourselves in life—a job interview, giving a speech, an exotic trip, or retirement—but seeing your parent in an open casket is not one of them. Don't get me wrong. I had seen *many* open caskets in my lifetime. In fact, I had *kissed* the dead people *in* the open caskets. My Ukrainian grandmother Buni taught me to kneel solemnly at the casket, touch the deceased's cold neatly folded hands, pray, weep, and then kiss the person on the cheek. You read that correctly. *Kiss* the dead person! I had the privilege of doing this with my grandfather, great-grandmother, and a half dozen other relatives all before I was ten years old! I was well trained in ethnic funeral parlor protocol.

But no matter how well funeral parlor-trained we are, every part of the internment process is awkward, including having to pick out the outfit in which your beloved person will be buried. I stood in my mother's closet thinking, "In what did she look prettiest?!" And I was under the gun; the funeral parlor men were there waiting, impatiently I might add. I picked a floral silk blouse that had perfect hot and light pinks and a hint of peach. When my mother was healthy and wore this blouse, she was beautiful.

I answered a dozen questions along the way to burial about the casket, prayer cards, tombstone, flowers, and pallbearers, but I

Pink, Berry, Plum Maybe, but Never Peach

never thought I had to be bold enough to pick lipstick color. And I wish I had.

It is a ridiculously surreal experience when friends and family come together to mourn your loved one. And God bless all the people who said, "She looks good!" which begs the question, of course, by what standard really? She looks better than other dead people? Do any of them actually look good? They all look dead and made over, and in my mother's case, a makeup job horribly flawed! From an embalmer's perspective, the work was top notch. From a 1980s *Color Me Beautiful* perspective, she was wearing peach lipstick, and peach was *not* her color.

I panicked, found the nearest Kleenex, and then irrationally wiped that horrible peach smear off her lips. I don't know what color stay lipstick brand funeral parlors use, but this color barely budged. I quickly disposed of the tissue evidence, simultaneously realizing my mother now lay without lip color, which does nothing for a dead person. I had not fully thought out my plan. As if my arm were not a part of my body, I thrust my hand into my purse and found my *berry* lipstick. Yet another life lesson: applying lipstick to a dead person is not easy. Apparently, lipstick melts onto warm lips more easily than cold ones. And I was absolutely rushing because heaven forbid the funeral parlor staff see me repainting their canvas!

My mother would not have approved of my lipstick efforts; they were sloppy at best. But I always say, "God does not expect us to be perfect, but he expects our intentions to be perfect." My intentions, in that peach-tinted moment, were sadly and genuinely perfect.

27
Operation Comfort Food

THERE ARE CERTAIN FOODS that are simply synonymous with your mother or father, or whoever that person is who fed and sustained your being for so long. These are the foods that comfort us and bring us back to those infancy and toddler stages when our mother smelled like the foods she cooked as we hugged her. To surviving preteen and teenage years when we had one foot in childhood and one foot in young adulthood and weren't quite sure where we belonged, and we really needed calories to manage the raging hormones. To those young adult years when we started to realize if we didn't start cooking for ourselves, we would physically starve! And at each stage, all we wanted was comfort food. For me it was *pyrohy*, which are Ukrainian potato and cheese dumplings, which I love most with butter and sauteed onions.[1] It would take my mother days to prepare them, and they were inhaled at the kitchen table in record-breaking time. My sister and I would race to see who could eat more on Christmas Eve, which would simultaneously exasperate my mother and make her beam with pride. I have a deep love for her chocolate pistachio cake, which is super moist and delicious, and her *paklava*, which is an Armenian delicacy of phyllo dough, nuts, sugar and cinnamon, with enough butter to clog each of your arteries five times over. And my all-time favorite

---

1. Many ethnicities share a similar delicacy to Ukrainian *pyrohy*, like Polish *pierogis* or Russian *vareniki*.

Operation Comfort Food

dessert: heart-shaped cut out cookies (the secret ingredient is sour cream) with the perfect pink glaze! But when the person who provided those comfort foods for your entire life is no longer with you, there is a void that takes your breath away and makes you wonder if you will ever eat again. Dramatic? Yes. True? Also, yes. And so, I felt this life sustaining responsibility to preserve my mother's recipes—Operation Comfort Food began.

My mother was obsessed with cooking. She had close to one hundred cookbooks, even more magazines and index cards, all chock full of recipes she had tried or planned to try. And every recipe had handwritten notes on it—changes she had made, things she might add or delete from the recipe in the future, and when and to whom she served the recipe. And *none* of it was organized in the very least. Don't get me wrong, my mother was truly Type A and very organized. But you can appreciate how a recipe collection grows! And when you are an amazing cook like my mom, your recipes are written down with assorted notes, but your recipes are also half-memorized. Consequently, I was faced with the challenge of organizing it all and preserving our family's favorites. I spent time going through each cookbook to find the pages she had marked, and I would photocopy the recipe and then toss the book because I was desperately trying to eliminate the clutter.

At the start of every month, my mother would sit and make a list in an old-fashioned stenographer's notebook of all the recipes she wanted to cook during that month. She was so dedicated to providing healthy and delicious meals for my dad, my sister, and me that by hook or by crook, she stuck to that list. Take-out food was a treat that happened once a month at best. So, in this recipe preservation process, I would look through her years and years of monthly menu notebooks and then search to find the recipe in the assorted books or scraps of paper to make sure it was preserved. I also found an entire recipe card box filled with over one hundred index cards with handwritten menus she had planned for every event she had ever hosted since she was married in 1967! She hosted bridge groups, church groups, family, friends, holidays, super bowl parties, post-wedding brunches, and birthdays. The list was long! Each card included details about the centerpiece, specialty cocktail, appetizers, main dish, salad, vegetable, and dessert, along with the occasion and the people with whom she had socialized. My favorite notes were her reminders to herself to fill the candy bowl or put fresh towels in the bathroom. My favorite card was from a time she was clearly hosting family for ten days. She had elaborate menus for each day and then on day five she wrote "take-out pizza." It was her breather to get through the remaining five days! Reading these menus was emotional and affirming at the same time; I realized from whom I had been trained.

I dumped a good few hundred dollars into the copy machine at the local Kinko's. But my final product was an index and collection, in two massive binders of every recipe my mother had repeatedly cooked. The grand total was over five hundred recipes! I imagine in the event of a house fire I would instinctively grab those two binders on my way out the front door. Why? Those recipes reflect a lifetime of creativity, hard work, nurture, and love, and a legacy I need to preserve and share with my children. Life sustaining comfort food because a girl has to eat, right?!

28

Planting Trees

WHEN LIGHTNING THE GUINEA pig died (he was named after Lightning McQueen in the movie *Cars*, because he was faster than fast!) we desperately worked to find a way to preserve his memory for our seven-year-old son Matthew, who was genuinely devastated. We held a memorial service in the backyard, and standing in a circle, each family member had the opportunity to share a special memory about this small, hilarious, and adorable rodent. We painted a rock to mark where Lightning was buried in the backyard, and we put a photo of Matthew holding Lightning (when he was youthful and alive) in a beautiful wooden frame for him to keep on the nightstand in his bedroom. We did what we could to acknowledge the loss and put in place memorials so Lightning would never be forgotten. And we similarly memorialized Hilton the Beta Fish (got him at an auction that was held in a Hilton hotel), Guinness the cat (exact color of the beer), two dwarf hamsters (Chester and Winnie), Shamu the cat (he really did look like the whale), and a good half-dozen hermit crabs, each with distinct personalities.

There is no limit to the creative and assorted ways humans memorialize pets, family members, and friends who have passed away, and for good reason. Memorials are our attempt to celebrate the life that has been lived, loved, and lost and put in place reminders of that person or animal who has passed, so we never forget them. And deep down, we can all acknowledge our secret wish that one day people will memorialize us as well, because the idea of being forgotten is, for lack of a better word, sad.

And so, when my mother passed away, my children knew the drill, and we worked quickly to memorialize their grandmother. Our family, with the help of our ministers, planned a meaningful memorial service; we shared a plethora of photos that spanned my mother's lifetime; the sanctuary choir beautifully sang her favorite anthem; we filled bowls with her favorite flavored jellybeans for everyone to enjoy; her grandchildren recited Psalm 23, my mother's favorite Bible verse (and there was not a dry eye in the church); we eulogized my mother, sharing favorite memories and celebrating her incredible life; our minister preached a beautiful meditation;[1] we walked from the church sanctuary to the historic cemetery down the hill and stood together with friends and family as her casket was lowered into the ground; and we each tossed a flower into the earth before we departed. It was just like Lightning the guinea pig's memorial, on a slightly larger scale.

When my mother passed away, the school my mother taught at for fifteen years (ECLC of New Jersey) reached out immediately with wonderful sentiments about my mother and beautiful testimonies from students and parents who loved "Mrs. N." And the ECLC family memorialized my mother in beautiful and unexpected ways. With contributions my mother's colleagues, friends and family made in her memory, the school created the Barbara Nahabedian Scholarship for a graduating senior, which I know would make my mother equally humbled and proud. She would love that something good was coming out of something bad, and that her students were continuing to benefit from her legacy as a teacher, even after she was gone. The school also planted a tree on the campus in memory of my mother, with a beautiful plaque commemorating her time and dedication to the school. This gesture was the greatest gift to our family. The dedication of the tree at the school was a very special and personal ceremony that helped our family in the early stages of the healing process.

---

1. See Appendix E for the meditation preached by our pastor, Sean Miller.

Planting Trees

ECLC is an accredited, non-profit school that educates students ages five to twenty-one with autism spectrum, Down syndrome, severe learning and/or language disabilities, or multiple disabilities. My mother *loved* teaching there and would not have wanted to be anywhere else. That speaks volumes of the school, its teachers and staff, and its students. It also speaks volumes about my mother. People have often asked me what exactly my mother loved about teaching. I assume it's that she loved making a difference in the life of a child; that she was able to build children up and make them feel better about themselves; and that she had confidence in them and helped them realize their potential, even when challenged by physical, mental, economic, and emotional disabilities. My mother, perhaps because of her upbringing and the environment from which she came, was the person always looking out for the underdog; she taught my sister and me to look around a room and first and foremost find the person who most needed a friend. I am reassured by the fact that this is what my mother did for fifteen years at ECLC: look around the room and find the student who most needed a friend.

My mother was the teacher who came home from work, cooked dinner for her family, threw in a load of wash, sorted the mail, paid a few bills, did odd tasks around the house, and then sat down to school-related work until she fell asleep exhausted at the kitchen table. She was the teacher who had an individualized classroom and homework plan for every student, writing out personally tailored worksheets for each of her fifteen students. She was the teacher who found prom dresses for students at her school who could not afford them, who baked a cake for each of her students on his or her birthday in case the student did not get one at home, and who brought in guest assistants to help tutor students in areas she knew they had a special interest, like building model airplanes. Barbara was the teacher who had her students fill out success logs at the end of each day, recording at least one accomplishment, success, or something he or she did well that day; who walked with them into town so they could practice life skills in stores and restaurants;

Scratch My Itch

and who helped her students organize their campaigns when they were running for student government offices.

My mother retired from ECLC at the end of the school year in 2010; she had fallen on the sidewalk at school in the spring of that year, and we all assumed it was courtesy of uneven pavement. We did not know it was a harbinger of things to come. She retired from teaching, putting away her writing paper with the red baseline and broken blue midline, the detailed academic planner, colorful bulletin board borders, red pens, motivational stickers, and laminating machine. She was looking forward to spending more time with her husband, her daughters, sons-in-law, and grandchildren; more time working on needlepoint and cooking; and more time relaxing and living life to its fullest without school hours and a long commute encroaching on her daily schedule. Following her spring retirement, she enjoyed a summer knowing she would not have to head back to school in the fall, only to receive a diagnosis of ALS that Labor Day weekend.

Given this context, you can begin to appreciate the significance to our family of the Scholarship Fund and the planting of a tree on the school grounds in her memory. The school acknowledged the commitment she had made to her students for so many years and celebrated all she had represented and accomplished. Having other people unexpectedly memorialize the person you love is just an amazing thing. The company my husband works for also gifted us a tree when my mother passed away—a beautiful red bud that is planted in our backyard. We call it "Babi's Tree," and while this tree has lost limbs and bends at a funny angle, it continues to grow and bloom every year and is also a loving reminder of my mother.

As I meditate on the idea of a memorial tree, I cannot help but think about the incredible symbolism a tree, or any living plant, imparts when a person we love has passed away. I doubt there is a more perfect memorial. As the tree takes root, it struggles to establish itself in its new place, and then over time it steadily grows and blossoms. The tree may lose limbs or leaves, it may bend at funny angles, but it grows and lives. After a loved one has passed away, don't we too struggle to establish ourselves in our new place, a place that is without the person we lost? And, like the tree, in our struggle we eventually take root, and we continue to grow maybe in ways we did not expect and with challenges akin to losing limbs and leaves. But we live, and over time, hopefully we bloom. Our prayer is that the memory and legacy of the person we love, as embodied in a tree, will be there as a reminder to us, for the next generation and the generation after that, that life goes on. And we all secretly hope one day, we too will not be forgotten. And I fully expect when our cat Cleo (her eyes look like Ancient Egypt's Cleopatra) passes away one day, we will be planting yet another tree; we have grown to love this memorial tradition.

> The other day I looked on the ECLC of New Jersey website and found out the teacher from ECLC, Mrs. Nahabedian, had ALS and passed away this past June. So sad. That was so very nice of you and the rest of the ECLC staff to plant a flower for Mrs. Nahabedian. Everyone will miss Mrs. Nahabedian so much. It's so very sad. She was a very kind and wonderful lady.
> —Email to the school principal from one of my mother's former students

29

Searching for Heaven

SOMETIME AFTER MY MOTHER passed away, after the funeral had been held, the thank you notes written, the casseroles eaten, and her closet cleaned out, I was left to wonder. And wonder I did. And in addition to wondering, I started looking for evidence of where she was now. Proof that what I believe is actually true. As a Christian, I say I walk by faith and not by sight, but really, all I wanted in a clinical crazy sort of way was to "see." Faith sounds nice, and I had relied on it my entire life and had rarely doubted it. But now I needed evidence. I needed to know my mother, in leaving this physical world, had gone to heaven to be with God our maker and that really, it was so unbelievably amazing that she was not missing me in the very least. At least, not to the degree I was missing her.

So, where to find evidence? Barnes and Noble, of course. I went on a spending spree and started reading books that substantiated there is a heaven. Not just one book or two books but *multiple* books (six to be exact). Books written by people with near-death experiences. Books written by people who claimed they clinically died and came back to life. Books written by people who died, came back, died again, and came back again. A researcher by training, I was looking for consistency in their stories. There is statistical power based on sample size, and I was looking for a large enough sample size of books to convince me my mother was indeed where I believed her to be, supported by the vast evidence of people who had been to heaven and had come back to earth. This was a fun and slightly costly experiment that kept me busy for a while. And then I gave it a rest. Research can be draining. And I decided I would walk by faith and prayed what I believed was true.

But then, I started looking for signs my mother's spirit was in a good place (heaven, ideally), or dare I say, stuck in our house? She did die here. I started to doubt my thoughts about heaven and started wondering about a person's spirit being stuck where that person died, also known as "haunted." There were a series of things in our house that were just a little funny in the first few weeks after my mother's death. There was the time my oldest daughter said she woke up at 4:00 in the morning because someone had turned her bedroom lights on! She said she had to get up out of bed, walk clear across the room, and turn the lights off (side note: 4:00 am is when we estimated my mother passed away). Or the time my son could not find a small beloved toy, and he scoured his room, searched the house, interrogated his sisters who swore up and down they had no idea where his toy was, and this toy was nowhere to be found. And then I had this strange feeling and like in a tiny whisper, heard the words "look under his pillow," and there it was! It was just the kind of prank my mother would have pulled on my son, who is a total smartass, if she could have. And then there were the times I would listen on the baby monitor in my bedroom and hear, in my youngest daughter's bedroom, sounds of someone moving things around. And yet no one was up in the room. When I would go into the room to look, the hairs on my arm would stand up. And I wondered about these things because my mother was never able to get upstairs to the kids' rooms because of her illness. When she was sick, I took videos of their bedrooms to show her since she could not get to the second floor of the house. She would say many times during her illness how she wished she could see their rooms. And so, after she passed away, and these weird things were happening, I had to wonder if my mother was finally getting to the second floor! And the light in my bathroom shower. I was convinced she was playing with it until my husband brought in an electrician who said the connection was bad, replaced it, and the light no longer

Scratch My Itch

flickered. That ruined my shower conversations with my mother. I then gave up searching for evidence.

Sleuthing ceased but praying did not. My continued prayer was reasonably direct and simple: "Please God, a sign." I assumed at this point in time, God was rather bored with my monotonous petition. And sometimes, in dire frustration, I would circumvent God entirely and talk directly to my mother, usually with a little more anger and attitude. My New Jersey came out, and the prayer would be a little more like, "Why the hell have you not sent me a sign?!" Looking back, maybe the swearing was not helping my cause.

But then. It was a normal morning. I was in my bathroom getting ready to start my day, and I was humming a tune. I woke up humming it. And I asked myself, "what song is this I am humming?" Mascara brush wand in hand, I was talking to myself in the mirror and was genuinely confused. And I had this overwhelming feeling about my mom. I was so confused I brought my husband into the internal conversation I was having with myself. "Paul, what is this tune I am humming?" and then, I hummed it for him. He replied, "I don't know." It was early, and neither of us was truly invested in the conversation or the tune. But as I continued getting ready, I was still hearing the melody in my head and thinking about my mom. It would not go away, and as if I were in a cartoon, it got louder and louder. Then, mid-makeup application, I got a word: "ramble." A clue? And then "eagles fly." Another clue?! I quickly got up from my vanity chair (complete understatement folks, I flew), walked clear across the house in my bra and panties to the laundry room where my computer is and typed "ramble, eagles fly, song" into Google. I then clicked on a link that made me cry from the deepest part of my soul. The song is called "Corner of the Sky" from the musical *Pippin*, about a man searching for happiness (aren't we all!). When I listened to it, I recalled the tune for sure. I heard it back when I was a young child in the 1970s, but I certainly did not recall the lyrics. As I listened to Diana Ross sing the song on a YouTube video, I cried harder than any other time during my mother's illness and death. The line that struck me especially was "I don't fit in anywhere I go," which was something my mother

Searching for Heaven

had said repeatedly to me during her lifetime. Her South Boston immigrant-infused childhood, factory-adjacent rowhouse living, sexual abuse trauma—it all cast shadows that made it challenging for her to feel truly comfortable and safe in life. Listening to Diana Ross, it was as if my mother were singing the song.

> Rivers belong where they can ramble
> Eagles belong where they can fly
> I've got to be, where my spirit can run free
> Gotta find my corner, of the sky
>
> Everything has its season
> Everything has its time
> Show me a reason
> And I'll soon show you a rhyme
> Cats been on the windowsill
> Children fit in the snow
> Why do I feel I don't fit in anywhere I go
>
> Rivers belong where they can ramble
> Eagles belong where they can fly
> I've got to be, where my spirit can run free
> Gotta find my corner, of the sky
>
> Every man has his daydream
> Every man has his goal
> People like the way dreams have of
> Sticking to the soul
> Thunder clouds have their lightning
> Nightingales have their song
> And can't you see I want my life
> To be something more than long
>
> Rivers belong where they can ramble
> Eagles belong where they can fly
> I've got to be, where my spirit can run free
> Gotta find my corner, of the sky
>
> So many men are destined to settle for something small
> But I won't rest

Scratch My Itch

'till I know I have it all
So don't ask where I'm going
Just listen when I'm gone
Far away you'll hear me singing
Softly to the dawn

Rivers belong where they can ramble
Eagles belong where they can fly
I've got to be, where my spirit can run free
Gotta find my corner, of the sky

 Her life ended early at sixty-nine. Couldn't I see she wanted her life to be something more than long? "Don't ask where I am going. Just listen when I'm gone. Far away, you'll hear me singing softly to the dawn." From that moment on, I stopped searching for evidence. I stopped asking if my house were haunted. I stopped wondering where my mother's spirit was. I knew. She found her corner of the sky. And instead, I kept praying—but a different prayer this time. A prayer that one day, I would find that same corner, so I could be with her again.

30

Postscript
Stitch by Stitch

I AM THE QUEEN of unfinished projects. When I was young, my modus operandi was having an idea of something I wanted to create, and then beginning without a fully thought-out plan. Invariably I would run into roadblocks, and I would either get frustrated, distracted, or inspired by something else and start a new creative project without having finished the first one. As a child, I could have opened a fantastic museum of creative unfinished projects! As an adult, I am now *much* better at completing projects; however I am usually working on *many* projects simultaneously. For example, right now, in addition to writing this book, I am crafting a cool serving tray using old Bazooka Gum comics from when I was a kid, compiling a cookbook for my children filled with recipes and family stories, completing a needlepoint piece, and making a quilt from my grandmother's old embroidery and fabric scraps. It's good to have many irons in the fire, right? What I have learned about myself is sometimes I am in the mood to work on one project and sometimes I am in the mood to work on another. Variety is indeed the spice of life! The tragedy, of course, is if you pass away before your multiple projects are complete.

The apple does not fall far from the tree. When my mother passed away, I inherited *six* of her partially stitched needlepoint

Scratch My Itch

pieces. I could not throw away my mother's unfinished work, but rather, I felt this overwhelming need to complete it for her. In an unexpected way, even though she is not with me, I feel close with my mother while stitching. Holding a canvas I know she held, admiring the colors of thread I know she personally picked out, squeezing the needle between my fingers in the same way my mother did, and finishing a design I know she loved makes me happy. With each stitch, I can hear my mother reminding me to make the back of the canvas look as neat as the front and to make sure my X's are consistently taut and the threads are all crossing in the same direction. In working on my mother's canvas, unlike my own, I am not cutting corners. If I make a mistake, I can't and don't keep going. Rather, I end up removing the entire row of bad stitching and doing it over. Finishing my mother's work and making sure it is done the way she would have done it is forcing me to slow down and be patient, to enjoy every time the needle goes into the canvas and then back up and out, and to honor her in the work I am doing.

Since my mother passed away, I have finished three of her six unfinished pieces. The first piece I completed was a whimsical needlepoint in muted colors of a vintage teddy bear wearing an equally vintage looking necktie with the words "This seat is reserved." My mother had dreamed of making it into a pillow for my father's reading chair, and so that is where the bear now sits, stuffed and with a beautiful navy velvet backing. The second piece, a detailed sampler with rich colors and intricate patterns, is now framed and hanging on my father's living room wall, his personal art gallery collection featuring Barbara's lifetime work. Most recently, I finished a Christmas bell pull my father now hangs on his door during that most wonderful time of year. Leave it to my mother to challenge me from beyond the grave. I first had to learn what a bell pull was (they originated in the Victorian era), then finish the needlepoint, purchase the materials needed to transform the needlepoint into a bell pull, and finally use my sewing machine to bring it all home. Challenge accepted and completed. I finally conceded the fourth needlepoint piece was too difficult and

Postscript

way beyond my skill set, and so I asked one of my mother's best girlfriends who also loves to stitch to please complete it on my mother's behalf. Sometimes it takes a village. While I have loved the stitching experience itself, it is the happy expression on my father's face when he opens a package with a tag that reads "To Charlie, Love Barbara," as if she were somehow gifting from the heavens, that makes the stitching something I want to do. However, as my farsightedness gets worse with age, the magnifying glass has become my new best friend, and the fact that my mother selected Aida and linen with the most squares possible per inch, I imagine it will take me the rest of *my* life to finish stitching the remaining two pieces.

Like the unfinished embroidery I am completing, so do our hearts knit themselves back together stitch by stitch after tragedy. We can still see the seams where there were tears in our hearts, and the sleek cotton floss holding the seams together may be of assorted colors each representing a different time in life when we felt true sadness, but that is what makes a person's heart even more interesting and beautiful. Since my mother passed away, I have learned one way our hearts are knit back together is by remembering special days and anniversaries and finding moments and activities to honor the person we love who has passed away.

At Christmas, which coincides with my mother's birthday, and at Easter, we always contribute to the flowers at church in my mother's memory because it feels as if the red poinsettias and fragrant Easter lilies are whispering to my mother, "well done, thou good and faithful servant." On the first anniversary of my mother's passing, I wrote her a letter (see Appendix F), a wish list, with all the sentiments that were still weighing on my heart a year later. It was helpful to take pen to paper, and I felt the same freedom and relief when as a young girl, I would write "Dear Diary, . . ." Also on that first anniversary, our family bought a bunch of white helium balloons (yes, I know they are potentially dangerous for birds and marine life . . .), and we each wrote our personal message to Babi in black Sharpie on our balloon and then together released our helium-filled sentiments into the heavens, hoping for express delivery. These are examples of a just few small gestures our family has made to honor my mother's memory as we learn to live without her. I would love to hear the creative and loving ways in which you have honored those who have come before you. I firmly believe little acknowledgements and speaking aloud that person's name and honoring their legacy is what helps us remember the past but also enables us to live in the present with hearts that are gently stitched back together. May it be that way for you, for me, and for all those we love.

> I guess the thing about faith is just that, it is faith. And maybe God is sending us "signs" daily, but we are just too busy or ignorant to recognize them. It makes me think of Samuel and Eli. God was basically yelling at Samuel, and it wasn't until Eli told him it was the Lord calling that he realized what was going on. God may not send an angel with a certified, handwritten message from your Mom, but maybe it is things like your Mom's friend having the ability to complete your mother's cross stitch [that she did not finish] so beautifully that tells you everything is *complete* and your mom is in a beautiful place with her Savior.
> —Email a friend sent to me

Postscript

"What you leave as a legacy is not what is etched into stone monuments, but what is woven into the lives of others."—Anonymous

Appendix A
Caregiver Bill of Rights[1]

THE ALS ASSOCIATION SHARED this *Caregiver Bill of Rights* with me during my mother's illness. At the time, hearing words that advocated for the caregiver, and not only for the person needing care, was a gift to me, and I would occasionally return to this bill of rights over three years to remind myself what was considered okay in caregiving land. If you are a caregiver, I hope this bill of rights will also offer you some guidance and reassurance as you provide care to your loved one. I have the right to:

- Take care of myself. This is not an act of selfishness. It will give me the capacity to take better care of my loved one.

- Seek help from others even though my loved one may object. I recognize the limits of my own endurance and strength.

- Maintain facets of my own life that do not include the person I care for, just as I would if he or she were healthy. I know that I do everything that I reasonably can for this person, and I have the right to do some things for myself.

- Get angry, be depressed, and express other difficult feelings occasionally.

---

1. ALS Pathways, "Caregiver Bill of Rights."

Appendix A

- Reject any attempt by my loved one (consciously or subconsciously) to manipulate me through guilt, anger, or depression.

- Receive consideration, affection, forgiveness, and acceptance for what I do for my loved one for as long as I offer these qualities in return.

- Take pride in what I am accomplishing and to applaud the courage it has sometimes taken to meet the needs of my loved one.

- Protect my individuality and my right to make a life for myself that will sustain me in the time when my loved one no longer needs my full-time help.

- Expect and demand that as new strides are made in finding resources to aid persons in our country, similar strides will be made toward aiding and supporting caregivers.

Appendix B
The Original Lecture

MOM AND DAD,

A few thoughts from your daughter who loves you both very much and equally:

1. Currently, in your marriage, there are *two* people who are sick. While you may disagree with me, one of you is *not* more tormented than the other. You both have diseases for which there is no cure, which is maddening. You both have and continue to receive treatments in hopes of making things better. It is *equally hard* being the caregiver *and* the care receiver. *Your sorrow, for yourselves and one another, is equal.* This is not a competition to see whose situation is worse. You both win. Your situations both are different but equally painful.

2. You must *listen to one another* and respect what that person requests—heck, anticipate the other person's needs and do it before he or she asks! This is what makes a marriage. For example, if Dad says he is tired and would like to go to bed early, you, Mom, should bend over backwards to make sure that happens. He is suffering. In the same way, Dad, if Mom asks you to please leave the computer for a period of time so you can focus on something important to both of you, think

Appendix B

about priorities and spend time together. If you both put the other person first, then it's a win-win for you both.

3. You must each *be flexible*. This means that if the schedule gets messed up for the day, you go with it! It means Dad, if you don't get to respond to every email because Mom's doctor appointment went longer than expected, you realize the world does not stop turning because you don't respond until the next morning. It means if Dad gets held up at the National Institutes of Health and comes home exhausted, you say to him, "I understand you are tired Charlie, so let's just do my shower tomorrow instead of tonight." Flexibility is a gift that is *so* appreciated by the other person.

4. Things cannot be perfect. *"Good enough" is okay!* Please leave your perfectionism, obsessions, and compulsions at the door. It is hard enough to maintain high standards when everything in life is peachy keen. It is unbearable trying to meet expectations of perfection when operating at half a tank of gas. Both of you need to lessen your expectations of the other and lighten up. If things get done differently than you would do it, it does not make it wrong.

5. Dad, if Mom's demands are making you angry, please remove yourself from the situation and ask for help. Ask me, Theresa, Paul, anyone. Walk away. *No being rough. It will not be tolerated.* Medications can and will make you not be in control of your emotions, and we all need to recognize this and not bury our heads in the sand. It is for your safety and mom's safety. If we need to get extra help on those days we know you are going to be less patient and more grouchy, that is a wise investment.

6. *Being ill or disabled does not excuse you from being gracious and polite*—with one another, and with people who are here to help you. I do not care how bitter, angry, tormented, or miserable you are, a simple please and thank you goes a long way.

The Original Lecture

7. *Mom,* it is important you have Theresa, or whichever other caregiver is here, do *as much as possible,* and have Dad do *as little as possible,* with your basic care needs. This is important for you and for him. The less Dad is your primary caregiver, the more he can be your husband. Please understand that *fewer than 1 percent* of husbands would be doing *half* of what you expect and ask Dad to do. Most husbands would have given you over 100 percent to someone else's care or would have *walked out.* Multiple home health aides have told me this. My own husband would never do half of what Dad is doing, nor would I ask or want him to. You need to rely on caregivers to tend to your basic needs and let Dad be there to be your friend, partner, and confidant.

8. *Dad,* you need to work on better time management. There are a set number of hours in the day. And in your day, you need to balance time spent on work and time spent on doing things with mom that are mutually agreeable to you. My suggestion is each day, you set aside an hour or so when you and Mom work on something both of you want or need to do. That time is uninterrupted. This means, you let your phone calls go to voicemail, you don't walk by your computer and get caught up in emails. You focus on what you and mom want to do. And in each day, you set time aside when you are working on your job's work. And this means during that hour or so, you don't get interrupted. Mom, you must rely on the other caregiver 100 percent during that time, so Dad can focus and give his work 100 percent of his attention.

9. *You must treat caregivers with respect.* This goes back to being polite. You certainly can and do decide who you retain and don't retain with respect to the people taking care of you. You must remember, however, that the caregivers *too* have a choice. If they don't like you, because you are rude, inconsiderate, or overly demanding, they can just as easily choose *not* to be here. While there are caregivers who are not as smart, educated, or efficient as you, it does not make you a better

Appendix B

person than they are. Lose the attitude and appreciate that these people are trying to work to earn a living and are not in a very glamorous job. Appreciate the job they do because you need them. You would never want to do the job they are doing.

10. *Dad*, it is time for a *hearing aid*. *Mom*, it is time for you to use an *amplifier*. This will go a long way in helping everyone with communication. It is also a safety issue. Dad, you need to be able to hear Mom without her straining herself. Mom, everyone else, including health aids, needs to be able to hear you from one side of the lower level to the other without your straining too much. Safety first.

11. *The routine needs to change.* The day does not start at 8:00 p.m. when the home health aide leaves. No matter what you think. Dinner needs to be at 6:30 p.m., which is when the rest of the world eats. And you need to be in bed at 8:00 p.m. when Theresa or another health aide walks out the door. And then you can spend your evening in bed. This will relieve *much* stress on Dad who is left to get everything else done before he gets into bed. *Sleep is important.* Your bodies cannot possibly fight the diseases they have on little sleep. Let's be aware of the nights we know Dad will be excessively tired or impatient because of long treatment days and adjust accordingly. We can bring in extra help as needed, or we can be sure we are in bed extra early.

This is not easy for you Mom, for you Dad, or for me, to be honest. Watching your parents suffer is the most painful thing in the world. My love for you is immeasurable, and my job at this point is to make sure each of you is safe, well cared for, and able to continue to grow the love for one another that has carried you through almost forty-six years of marriage. Please talk together constructively and lovingly about the things I have brought up. I love you, Cyndy.

Appendix C

Anticipated Funeral Action Items

WHEN MY MOTHER WAS sick, I started a list of what I would need to do once she passed away. I love a good list of action items. With ALS, we knew how the story would end, and I am a planner, so it was not completely horrific my mind went where it did. I will tell you that on the day you celebrate the life of the person you have lost, with friends and family, no matter the size of the crowd, you will need a pack of tissues. And breath mints. You might even need a Xanax or a stiff drink. It is all okay. You will get through the very surreal day and ask yourself, "what exactly just happened?" later. You will feel the love of all the people who are there to support you. You will feel responsibility that comes with being the person who is left behind. You will find inner strength you did not know you had. And you will cry in the shower and in the car. I remember, after my mother's funeral, coming home and for the next few days (at least) feeling exhausted and numb. I could not comprehend what had just happened. Apparently, my mother died, and I buried her, had put on a luncheon, and visited, cried, and even laughed with family and friends. As you think through the action items on this list and then live through whatever grieving ceremony works for you, please be gentle with yourself, extend yourself grace, and take things one day at a time.

Appendix C

- Write obituary, select obituary photo, and decide where you would like it published.
- Obtain multiple copies of death certificate.
- Select funeral home and sign contract (select casket and plot or cremation).
- Plan visitation hours so family and friends can express condolences.
- Plan funeral/memorial/celebration of life service (Any special music offerings? Eulogy? Bible or other special readings?).
- If burial, select in advance in which outfit you would like your beloved person buried (be sure to remove any jewelry the person is wearing that you don't want buried).
- Where would you like donations in the person's memory to be made?
- Compile list of family and friends you will call/email to notify them of your beloved person's passing (it really helps to do this in advance).
- Write the eulogy.
- Order flowers for wake/funeral.
- Select pallbearers if necessary.
- Plan meal/refreshment for after the funeral/memorial/celebration of life service.
- Order pre-printed thank you note cards you can send to acknowledge people's donations, offerings, kind gestures, and condolences.
- Create slideshows of photos that can be shown during visitation hours or whenever family and friends gather.
- If you expect out-of-town guests, secure a block of rooms at a nearby hotel.

Appendix D
Eulogy

*By Cyndy Nahabedian Mamalian and
Christina Nahabedian Hanson*

(CYNDY READS) ON BEHALF of our father Charlie, Christina and I thank you all so much for being here today to celebrate our mother's life and for crying with us as we mourn her passing. We are truly humbled by your love and support, and our mother would be equally humbled.

The past three years have been exhausting for our family—physically, mentally, emotionally, and spiritually. We managed our mother's diagnosis of ALS, or Lou Gehrig's disease, with the overwhelming and frustrating understanding that there is no cure. But our mother had more than one cross to bear. Shortly after our parents moved to Maryland to be with us, Mom fell and suffered a spiral fracture to her leg. She never walked again. She was soon diagnosed with cancer and underwent radiation and chemotherapy for over a year, keeping this a secret from most everyone. She didn't like pity for sure. She then suffered from other medical challenges, including a blood clot and treatment for advanced stage Lyme disease. Through it all, our mother and family met up with almost every bad emotion out there—despair, pain, anger, anxiety, and frustration—but it was all peppered with humor and lots of love. Our mother's battle with ALS ended last Wednesday morning. To the very end, her mind was 100 percent intact and alive. She was still experimenting and trying to find a cure and praying for a miracle, but her body could no longer continue fighting this disease.

With all the hardship we have lived with as a result of this disease, it will truly take some time to turn our attention back to the good and to fully celebrate the person we knew our mom to be before this disease became her life—and our lives. But we need to start that process, and we need to start it now.

So, our mother . . .

She was gorgeous! And with such a set of legs and a dimpled smile . . . such a twinkle in her eyes . . . she was smart, feisty, talented, active, and stubborn—and a total compulsive Type A person! We learned to dust so no dust was left behind. We learned how to make hospital corners on our beds (in part due to Dad and his years in the Army), *but* we learned how to make a bed. We learned you only do your best, and nothing less. She was fastidious, particular about everything, and had very high standards. We quickly learned to work hard, challenge ourselves, and rise to the occasion, as we had high expectations to meet. Despite her high standards, she always made us feel special, and she was always looking for an occasion to celebrate. We learned family meant devotion and love. Mom instilled a love and appreciation for our ethnic culture and family history but first and foremost our faith in God. Mom was a very private person, and we learned to respect that.

Mom and Dad's devotion to one another: Mom and Dad loved each other since high school and college. Their love spanned the distance from Vietnam to the United States, and they were married after Dad returned from the war. I remember as a teenager finding love letters in their closet they had written back and forth when Dad was in Vietnam . . . They never went a day without writing to one another. Married in 1967, they were together for forty-six years. And Mom's favorite thing was dancing with Dad—ballroom dancing and Armenian line dancing. It was a love they shared.

Eulogy

(*Christina reads*) Mom and Dad showed us the perfect example of what it means to be equally yoked and truly committed to one another and in love. Let me tell you, Cyndy and I saw firsthand what it means . . . our mother always sacrificed for our father to make sure he was all he could be . . . and let us assure you, our father, until our mother's last breath, made sure she could be all that she could be. We have never seen greater devotion than what our father showed our mother over these past three years as she battled this disease. When she was the most frustrating ever, Dad would lovingly stroke her hair. And even when she could barely speak, she was looking out for him, making sure the placement of her oxygen tubing was not in such a location that he might trip over it and get hurt if he got up during the night. They flirted until the very end. Their love surpassed all understanding.

So, Mom's humble beginning . . . she came from blue-collar ethnic roots, her parents both worked in factories, and one of her goals in life was to make sure her girls understood what it meant to be "classy." She never wanted to go back to that from which she came. She grew up in a rowhouse with minimal plumbing. She wanted more for her children . . . and she was willing to work hard . . . and yet as hard as it was, that rowhouse was filled with love, and that love continued to the next generation. Learning from her own mother, she made sure we were always dressed tastefully, conservatively, and appropriately for every occasion, but that did not mean spending lots of money. She would sacrifice buying updated clothes for herself and shop at sales for us so we could have new dresses.

Our mom was a true artist, but her father told her she could become a teacher or a nurse. She couldn't stand the sight of blood, so she became a teacher. But she loved art, and her art classes, and she did end up doing art in other ways in her life: Ukrainian Easter eggs, needlepoint, knitting, stenciling, and quilting. She loved her years playing recorder with the Mendham Recorder Consort (and Cyndy and I remember the family photo of us all playing instruments as a family . . . I played the triangle!). We remember her sewing our clothes when we were little . . . matching outfits (I loved

Appendix D

being twins with Cyndy!) and eighth grade graduation dresses. As an adult, she and Dad loved singing in the church choir and ringing bells together. It was in their church choirs they felt absolute joy! And Mom encouraged Cyndy and me to excel in the arts. She drove me into New York City every week for six years so I could spend Saturdays at the School for Strings and Juilliard and paid for hours upon hours of music lessons, music camps, and recital dresses. It was a sacrifice she never questioned and truly enjoyed.

Mom (and Dad!) modeled hard work in so many ways. They were do-it-yourselfers, from mowing the lawn, gardening, weeding, planting new trees, harvesting and canning fruit and vegetables, cleaning, painting the house, wallpapering . . . we rarely saw Mom sitting down and relaxing because she always had a project to do. And as much as it was hard work, Mom and Dad always seemed to have fun doing it.

If there were just one word to define our mother, it would be "teacher." She taught before we were born, but stayed home with us while we grew up. So, after Cyndy and I were off to college, Mom went back and spent seventeen years teaching—she devoted 100 percent of herself to her special education students. She would spend the day at school working, would work after students left, would get home to cook dinner, and then was back to her schoolwork until very late into the early morning. She loved those children and made their lives her lives. We remember her looking for prom gowns for one of her students who could not afford one, and we remember her baking cakes for students whose parents she knew would not remember their birthdays. She was always volunteering, and yet as we grew up, she was ever present in our lives while we were in school. We still remember sitting at the kitchen table after school, often with milk and homemade cookies, talking about our day.

(*Cyndy reads*) So we have to talk about Mom's cooking—it is that on which she prided herself. We love the story of when she was first introduced to the Nahabedian family and she expressed interest in learning how to cook Armenian food, and one of the great aunts told her "it is too difficult for you, dear" . . . you don't

Eulogy

ever tell our mother something is too difficult for her. She learned how to make all our father's favorite Armenian dishes: *sarma, lehmajoun, yalenchi, tourshi, paklava,* and they even made string cheese. And our Dad would tell you our mom cooked it all better than all the old Armenian family! There are countless recipes my sister and I cook that are hers, and her homemade jams, jellies, and relish will truly be missed. She would always call and say, "I just tried this great new recipe! I'll put a copy in the mail to you with my notes since I made a few changes," which always turned out to be a laundry list of little ways she altered a recipe to make it better and make it hers. And she loved to entertain. We remember sitting at the top of the stairs when we were little when Mom and Dad were hosting dinner parties or bridge or Bible study groups, hoping we could get a glimpse of all the fun.

Our mother in her young mother years . . . she was a bit of tough love, and a lot of compassion and acceptance. She was our best friend, and we could tell her everything and anything. There are some stories we will never forget: the time Jeffrey Graham and I used bark chips to write all over the white siding of the house. The story goes that Mrs. Graham and our mother set out patio chairs and shared a glass of wine while Jeffrey and I were made to scrub down the house siding. Or when mom *literally* washed Christina's mouth out with soap for some bad language she tried on for size for the first time, or when she showed up at Christina's boyfriend's house because she stayed out past her curfew (she was grounded for two weeks, by the way). But Mom was our advocate. And she made sure we knew she was always in our corner. One last example is when the home computer crashed, and Christina lost her newly finished large term paper in her senior year of high school. Mom stayed up all night with her, sat by her side helping her rewrite what she had already written. It was pure support, sacrifice, and love.

And mom in her older years. She was a devoted grandmother who loved her grandchildren more than life itself. While she loved teaching, she secretly counted the minutes until she could retire to spend more time with her next generation of babies. She loved

Appendix D

Alexandra and Juliette for being girls, and she loved Matthew, Nicholas, Christopher, and Andrew for being the boys she never had. She marveled at their unique qualities and challenged them to be the best *they* could be.

(*Christina reads*) The disease our mom had is merciless, and it imprisons a person within their own body. Mom's mind through it all was a sharp as it always was . . . but she was trapped. For a person whose mind always raced, and whose body raced along too, this is maddening. For a perfectionist and someone with a mind for details—our mother until the day she died—you can start to imagine how beyond horrible this might be. Even at her end, she was still concerned with whether the sheets were without wrinkles and whether we were doing everything to the exact letter of the law. The demands were simple but painful very late at night. She tested our patience, and we had to keep reminding ourselves of all she had done for us—these should have been simple sacrifices for us.

Since she was diagnosed with ALS and experienced limited mobility, we started to mourn the loss of what could have been. She was a fighter, though, and rallied for her grandkids, attending Juliette's ballet recitals, Alex's horse shows, and Matthew's karate belt tests. She loved when Nicholas, Christopher, and Andrew would visit and make the house louder than usual! She made it to church most weeks and cried through the service even if she couldn't speak with people. We are grateful for those moments, as we like to believe those moments helped her spirit and strengthened her will to live.

Mom fought the good fight. And with this disease, that's all you can fight for—to live as much as you can even though you are slowly dying. Now we picture her in heaven enjoying a different retirement—not what she had planned but a peaceful one nonetheless. She will be singing, dancing (Alexandra says skipping!), and teaching the folks in heaven how to fold *cheese beureg* triangles, how to seal their *pyrohy* so they don't break open during boiling, and how to make the best homemade *lehmajoun*. And now she can be with her grandchildren in Texas and in Maryland, and with all of us, wherever we are in the world.

Eulogy

(*Cyndy reads*) My father, Christina, and I would like to extend a special thank you to all of you for your prayers, constant support, your emails and phone calls (most of which were never returned), for flowers sent, and prayer quilts made. We were so overwhelmed with the day-to-day care and challenges that we were often remiss in sending out that thank you note or making that phone call. Please know your expressions of love and support were *always* welcomed and met with tears in our eyes. We are also deeply grateful to all the caregivers who lovingly and patiently met our mother's needs: Theresa and countless others. Their arrival every day was a breath of fresh air, and we are deeply appreciative of their care and compassion. We are also truly appreciative of the ALS Association, the George Washington University Hospital Clinic doctors and professionals, and Montgomery Hospice, who held our hands as we endured this disease. We could not have done it without them.

A week or so ago, I had a dream while I was sleeping. Imagine a traffic circle in Europe. Cars driving quickly, everywhere. It was definitely a traffic circle, as cars merged and exited. It was chaos. And in the middle, I noticed someone was directing all the traffic. I realized it was our grandfather, our mother's father. He passed away when I was just eight years old and Christina was five, but I knew him well. I called out to him, "Gigi, Gigi, it is me, Cyndy, your granddaughter! We have not seen each other in a long while, but it is me!" His expression was recognition, but it was almost as if he didn't *want* to see me. He kept averting my gaze. I woke from a start from the dream, but his image was so real, so exact, the expressions, the movements, it haunted me the entire day. When I shared this dream with my friend Anna, she said, "Isn't it amazing to think that those who came before us are waiting for us." Those who came before us are waiting for us. As my friend Kristen said, "Cyndy, her father is calling her home." Mom did not get the retirement she dreamed of or deserved. She felt robbed of that time on earth. But Dad, Christina, and I believe she is with her parents again. That she is with all the saints in heaven. And it is on this faith that we must rest our hope and our trust.

Appendix E

Meditation

By The Reverend Sean Miller

"Great is thy faithfulness, O God my Father, morning by morning new mercies I see. All I have needed, thy hand hath provided. Great is thy faithfulness, Lord unto me."

IT IS A GREAT privilege and a humbling opportunity to be here today, and I am grateful to Pastor Bob for the invitation to share a few words this morning. Although I must say, I feel like I have known you Hilltop for a while now, for the last two years or so, since the first visit I had with Barbara and Charlie. At that first visit in their home in Potomac, Barbara insisted Charlie go and find the family albums, get them all out, so they could show me pictures of their family. Charlie did as he was told. And we sat, and enjoyed cookies and some iced tea, and soon enough, Barbara was talking about Cyndy's high school boyfriends and showing me pictures of Christina and Mark's wedding. But those weren't the first pictures that came out that day. The first pictures I saw of Barbara's family were pictures of the church choir and this church family she so

Meditation

loved. And then Charlie couldn't help but bring out the church cookbook Barbara helped to organize. So, it is a great privilege to be with you today, to put faces to a name of a church that was in every way the family whom she loved.

Barbara and Charlie were new members soon after I arrived [to Potomac Presbyterian Church] in the spring of 2011, and I realize I certainly did not know Barbara like many of you did as a teacher or as a choir member. But Barbara made quite an impression on me—as her pastor—not so much in long conversations we had, though we did share a few, but as time went on, those conversations became more difficult to have. But the impression Barbara made on me, and I think her whole church family in Potomac, was as it should be—just as St. Francis described how make an impression—how to convey the gospel—as he said, "Preach the gospel, but only, if necessary, use words."

So, I want to tell you what Barbara preached to me.

Barbara preached to me about dedication. Dedication to worship—I knew my sermons better be good because Barbara was there. Now, that isn't to say Barbara was critical of my sermons, but let me tell you: I was always so humbled when, just a few moments before church began, Charlie and Barbara would come in the front doors of the church. Because I knew the reality of her situation meant it was a struggle, sometimes a terrible struggle, just to get to church. Because Barbara was so dedicated to hear Cyndy singing in the choir, or to sit with Paul and Alex and Matthew and Juliette in their back center pew, being with her new church community, staying for fellowship even when that was really hard, too—it didn't matter.

Most Sundays if I had the chance to greet her coming out of worship, she would give me that smile—that expressive smile, sometimes just a glance, preaching without words about how glad she was to be in church with her family but how hard it had become, too. But those were weekly sermons that made the impression on her church community about dedication to her family and the family being together to worship together—you should have seen her Hilltop. You would have been so proud. You would have been so proud.

Appendix E

Barbara preached to me about music, too—a love we share. Because most Sundays when Barbara and Charlie would assume their center back pew, when the hymn would begin, I would often notice Barbara filling up with tears. Sometimes a few tears, but depending on the hymn, sometimes a lot of tears. And as Charlie would hold the hymnal for her, and as the hymn would continue, those tears were so expressive . . . perhaps it had been an extra challenging week, and those were tears of frustration, even anger. But more often than not, those tears would come from a deep well of faith—and those hymns she loved were so deeply meaningful to her because of what she felt and what she knew was true. Hymns that would express the ancient promise of God's faithfulness and love of Jesus Christ. Tears that shared a silent, but public, profession of faith in her Lord.

I didn't, and we at Potomac didn't know Barbara as you did, as the teacher, as the life of the choir party, but what God blessed us with was the Barbara we did know—who preached to us. She preached to me. She preached her gospel in the midst of what was, at times, an excruciatingly difficult journey. She preached her gospel with determination, even when it was hard for her to rely on others for help; she preached her gospel even up until this last Fourth of July, when Cyndy and Paul had a party during the afternoon and evening. Barbara was determined to be part of it. And I can't imagine how difficult it was to get her there that particular day, but something tells me nothing was going to stop her from being with the ones she loved, turning a Fourth of July backyard party into her sanctuary, friends into her congregation, the porch into her pulpit, and just her presence with us—her final and greatest sermon yet.

And what she has left us, her church family in Potomac, is that quiet legacy of dedication and faith—and I am grateful to God today that she left me a great collection of sermons—not the kind that are bound and put high up on a shelf in a pastor's study—no, these are the sermons Barbara left, the kind without words, the kind she left on my heart, on all of our hearts. Those are the ones people remember. Those are the ones we will remember. "Great is thy faithfulness, morning by morning new mercies I see. All I have needed, thy hand hath provided. Great is thy faithfulness, Lord unto me."

Appendix F

One Year Later
My Wish List

Dear Mom,

It has been one year since you passed away, and my heart is still breaking. I still cry when I think about you. I miss you desperately. I was thinking of my wishes—I have many in a day and I thought I would write a few down and share them with you.

- I wish you had never gotten sick.
- I wish your disease was one that could have been treated or had a cure.
- I wish you would talk to me, and I could hear your voice.
- I wish you could see Alexandra up on stage this coming weekend.
- I wish you were here for me to sit on your lap, to give you a hug, and have you hug me.
- I wish the end had not been so hard.
- I wish I had been with you when you passed away that early morning.
- I wish I had not found you dead.

One Year Later

- I wish you were here to keep Dad company and nag him when needed.
- I wish you were here so you and Dad could still flirt.
- I wish you and Dad were in your dream house, together.
- I wish you were here to cook your favorite meals.
- I wish you were here to call me to tell me about new recipes you tried and loved.
- I wish I could tell you all about my teaching the grade school students how to do Ukrainian Easter eggs.
- I wish you were here so I could complain to you, about anything. You always listened and cared.
- I wish I could talk to you about high schools for Alex.
- I wish you were here for your sense of humor.
- I wish you were here to love your cat, and so I could share animal stories with you.
- I wish I could talk with you about having a new teenager in the house.
- I wish I could ask you questions about menopause.
- I wish I could tell you we found wild raspberries on the side of the yard.
- I wish you were getting to enjoy your retirement, stitching and cooking.
- I wish we never had to deal with Hoyer Lifts, feeding tubes, medicines, ports, advance directives, "underwear," radiation burns, creams, gauze pads, bed pans, injections, and IV fluids.
- I wish you were here so I could put on your makeup for you and do your hair.
- I wish I could get you that glass of wine and feed you those jellybeans one at a time.
- I wish you had never lost the ability to walk, move your arms, speak, swallow, and breathe.

Appendix F

I wish your last words to me were not "help" and "morphine."

I wish I had talked to you in the end when I thought you were just sleeping.

I wish you could go to church on Sundays, effortlessly.

I wish people in Potomac had had the opportunity to get to know you in healthy times.

I wish you were here to swim in the pool and go to the beach.

I wish you were here to have seen Matthew get his first-degree black belt.

I wish you could see Juliette dance.

I wish you could see Pastor Sean and Sarah's new baby Hannah.

I wish I had been more patient and less frustrated.

I wish I had been more compassionate.

I wish I could just call you on the phone.

I wish I could tell you about how thankful I am that you were my mother.

I wish I could thank you for writing me letters every day when I was away at camp and a freshman in college.

I wish you were here to remember all the details of things Dad and I cannot remember, even when we put our heads together.

I wish you were here to see the changes we have made to the house.

I wish you could travel the world and see all the places you wanted to see but never did.

I wish you were here to help me sort through all the family photos and memorabilia.

I wish I could be sure I won't get ALS.

I wish I could tell you about new beauty products.

I wish I could cry with you.

One Year Later

- I wish you were here to hold a candle on Christmas Eve when we sing "Silent Night."
- I wish we didn't have to have purchased the handicap-accessible minivan.
- I wish we didn't have to have had home health aides in the house.
- I wish we never knew what the GWU ALS Clinic was.
- I wish we didn't have to have crushed pills.
- I wish you could see the girls in their dresses.
- I wish you could enjoy Matthew when he is charming and a real stinker.
- I wish I could hear you say, "I love you."
- I wish I could hear you say, "Cynd."
- I wish we had traveled and done fun things when you were only using a walker.
- I wish you could have gone with Dad on the church mission trip.
- I wish we could enjoy our glasses of wine on the back patio together.
- I wish I could call you when I wanted to brag about the kids, not because I like to brag, but only because I know you will be as excited as I am.
- I wish you were here to hear stories about my friends and their lives.
- I wish you were here to get excited about my elephant salt and pepper shakers.
- I wish you were here to appreciate the fact that I made *pyrohy*.
- I wish you could enjoy bourbon slush with me.
- I wish you were here to give me advice/nag me about my skin, my hair, my weight, and my clothes.
- I wish I could share my excitement with you over my first brand new washer and dryer ever.

Appendix F

I wish you were here to see horse shows, performances, soccer games, dance recitals, and karate belt tests.

I wish you were here so your grandchildren could love you.

I wish you could now tell me the meaning of life.

I wish you had not gotten sick.

I wish there was a cure for ALS.

I wish you were still here.

Mom, I miss you desperately. All my love, Cynd.

Bibliography

ALS Association. *Living with ALS Resource Guide: Approaching End of Life in ALS*. Arlington, VA: The ALS Association, 2022.

ALS Pathways. "Caregiver Bill of Rights." https://www.alspathways.com/caregiver-support/#know-your-rights.

Bunyan, John. *The Pilgrim's Progress*. New York: Barnes and Noble Books, 2005.

Dalai Lama, et al. *The Book of Joy*. New York: Avery, 2016.

The Episcopal Church. *The Book of Common Prayer*. New York: Church Publishing Incorporated, 1979.

Legally Blonde. DVD. Directed by Robert Luketic. Beverly Hills, CA: Metro-Goldwyn-Mayer; Universal City, CA: Marc Platt Productions, 2001.

National Institute on Drug Abuse. *Anabolic Steroids and Other Appearance and Performance Enhancing Drugs*. National Institute on Drug Abuse Research Topics. January 21, 2024. https://nida.nih.gov/research-topics/anabolic-steroids.

Oxford Languages. *Oxford Dictionaries Online*. https://www.oed.com/.

The Presbyterian Church, U.S.A. *The Presbyterian Hymnal: Hymns, Psalms, and Spiritual Songs*. Louisville, KY: Westminster John Knox, 1990.

"Stair." Merriam-Webster. https://www.merriam-webster.com/dictionary/stair.

Tutu, Desmond. *God Has a Dream: A Vision of Hope for Our Time*. New York: Image Books/Doubleday, 2011.

www.ingramcontent.com/pod-product-compliance
Lightning Source LLC
Chambersburg PA
CBHW062226080426
42734CB00010B/2039